HAGOP KEVORKIAN SERIES ON NEAR EASTERN ART AND CIVILIZATION

The publication of this work has been aided
by grants from The Hagop Kevorkian Fund
and The Andrew W. Mellon Foundation.

EGYPTIAN SAINTS

Deification in Pharaonic Egypt

Dietrich Wildung

New York · New York University Press · 1977

Copyright © 1977 by New York University
Library of Congress Catalog Card Number: 76-15147
ISBN: 0-8147-9169-7

Library of Congress Cataloging in Publication Data

Wildung, Dietrich.
    Egyptian saints.

    (Hagop Kevorkian series on Near Eastern art and
civilization)
    Includes bibliographical references and index.
    1. Gods, Egyptian. 2. Egypt—Religion. I. Title.
II. Series.
BL2450.G6W54 1977   299'.3'1   76-15147
ISBN 0-8147-9169-7

Manufactured in the United States of America

Contents

List of Illustrations

Foreword

It is a particular pleasure to introduce not only this splendid first volume in the *Hagop Kevorkian Series on Near Eastern Art and Civilization,* but also the series itself. New York University is deeply indebted to the Hagop Kevorkian Fund—for professorships, for a magnificent building, for libraries, and for very much else. In the long run, as a contribution to our knowledge of Near Eastern civilization, my belief is that the Hagop Kevorkian Lectureship in Near Eastern Art and Civilization and this *Series,* which will preserve the oral expression of the successive lecturers for reflective study and further research, will become a true symbol of the Fund's mission and a major part of the intellectual life of New York University. The intention of the university and more specifically of the Hagop Kevorkian Center for Near Eastern Studies is to invite annually a scholar of highest standard and who is currently engaged in significant research within the whole magnificent sweep of Near Eastern civilization—emphasizing artistic expression of various sorts—to deliver the lectures. The lectures will then be published in an ample form as illustrated in the current volume. Professor Dietrich Wildung's work, now complete, as well as the lectures already delivered by Professor Janine Sourdel-Thomine and Seyyed Hossein Nasr, which should appear in the series in coming months indicate that the high goals of those who administer the series will be realized and exceeded.

R. Bayly Winder, Dean
Faculty of Arts and Science
New York University

Preface

When most of us consider the Egyptian religion, we are inclined to look upon the gods of the pantheon as being immutable, pre-existing entities to serve the special needs of pharaonic theology. As it turns out, the Egyptians evolved and changed their gods over time; but we do not pay much attention to the process by which man creates his gods, and most of us have failed to appreciate the manner in which the Egyptians created theirs, as well. Basically, the gods that man creates are nothing else but the product of his reflection and religious feeling. Man conceives of and relies on his gods to explain experiences that otherwise would be unexplicable; man tries to deal with the problems which are raised by nature, by his daily life, and his inner life by personifying the powers behind them. Because these personifications are beyond any experience, they are therefore considered to be beyond any doubt. Often, the king assumes this personification of the supernatural and the superhuman powers. Unfortunately, the interrelationship of this supernatural being and the ordinary human takes place only within the narrow confines of the dogma of divine kingship. The divinity of the king is hidden behind temple walls and often may have little direct relevance for the people.

The Egyptians were among those who came to suffer estrangement from a superhuman authority they could rely upon to give help and advice with daily problems. The Egyptians did try in different ways to fill the religious vacuum that resulted. They created "popular editions" of the official gods, for example, the "Amun who hears the prayers" who was venerated at Karnak in the Unique Obelisk.[1] They also deified several ancient kings. Usually the people elevated and venerated local kings, and often comparatively briefly, in a rather informal, unorganized cult.[2] Thus, those living in western Thebes began to worship Amenophis I and his mother, Ahmes-Nefertari; they played an important role in the religious life of the common people.[3]

NOTES

1. Ch. F. Nims, in *Festschrift Ricke* (1971), 108, n.4.
2. D. Wildung, *Die Rolle ägyptischer Könige im Bewusstsein ihrer Nachwelt* (1969), for dynasties I through IV.
3. J. Cerný, *BIFAO* 27 (1927), 159–203; M. Gitton, *LdÄ* I, 102–109.

Introduction

Like the ale-wife who accompanied Gilgamesh, and the biblical sage Ecclesiastes, the unknown Egyptian author of the *Harper's Song* was highly skeptical about immortality. In the ancient Egyptian conception, a noble or "spirit" of the fargone past wasn't truly immortal unless he continued to be worshipped in the cult, which is to say that he was, in some sense, divine or deified. A true immortal was accessible to subsequent generations as an intercessor, as a channel bridging the gulf between the living and the dead.

The author of the *Harper's Song,* whose creation is preserved in several New Kingdom versions, counsels his reader (or listener) not to be preoccupied with immortality. He notes with disappointment that even the cult places of Imhotep and Hardjedef, both notables of the Old Kingdom, were in ruin and disrepair, nowhere to be found. If this was the case with respect to such great men of the past, whose skills and wisdom were celebrated, what hope was there for less gifted mortals? The lesson is clear: Concern yourself with life!

We may deduce from the *Harper's Song* that an ancient Egyptian fully expected that Imhotep would have been permanently worshipped at a cult place by virtue of his gifts, and not because he was a royal person. An even more obvious deduction is also evident: The author of the *Harper's Song* wrote at a time when Imhotep was not actively worshipped in Egypt. Had this poet lived in a later period, he might have been reassured by the resurgence of cultic activity related to Imhotep, who slowly but surely entered the pantheon of Egyptian deities, and was represented iconically in many temples and tombs.

Professor Dietrich Wildung carefully traces the process of Imhotep's entrance and acceptance in the Egyptian array of deities, over a period of millennia. He shows how the humane and creative abilities attributed to Imhotep, an architect and builder of the Old Kingdom and servant of Pharaoh Djoser, were mainly responsible for his ultimate deification, a process which was accelerated in the Greco-Roman period. What emerges is a composite personality.

In his introduction to the study concerning Imhotep, Professor Wildung provides a highly innovative interpretation to the general Egyptian concept of deification, attempting to correct some of the proverbial misconceptions about the divinity of the Egyptian Pharoah's. All in all, this volume, with its rich graphic documentation, affords a new perspective on Egyptian religion, as it was received and reinterpreted by the Hellenistic rulers of Egypt. Such historical investigations as this help to demonstrate that ancient Near Eastern civilizations represent a necessary area of study for Western man.

Baruch A. Levine
Professor of Hebrew
Department of Near East
Languages and Literature
New York University

EGYPTIAN SAINTS

Deification in Pharaonic Egypt

CHAPTER ONE

Sacred Kingship

As we shall see in the next chapters, the Egyptians elevated Amenhotep and Imhotep to the rank of saint and then god, in spite of the fact that Egyptian society was organized as a very strict hierarchy, operating according to very strict rules governing almost every aspect of life. These two individuals, and only a few others, had the qualifications to overcome the rules reserving supernatural qualities to the king. In contrast, most of the documents referring to Egyptian kings seem to indicate that the Egyptians almost routinely assumed that any pharaoh was a god. Actually, most of the texts and pictures we possess belonged to the privileged class, and most referred to the religious concerns of this same class of people, as well as to the domain of the dead, the funerary cult, and the afterlife. And, because the king was of their class, they would install him as a god automatically.

As I have just said, these documents pertain to the upper classes, and, for this reason, we should not rely upon them to any great extent to determine the religious practices of the common people, that is, to prove that the common people accepted any pharaoh as a god. This is illustrated by a study that two Frenchmen, Jules Baillet and Alexander Moret, made at the beginning of this century. They collected a large number of documents and quoted them to prove the divine character of pharaonic kingship.[1] Then, in 1960 Georges Posener

Fig. 1. Tomb of Ken-Amun at Thebes. The ram's horn at the king's
crown

published *De la divinité du pharaon,* in which he pointed out that these two scholars had made a one-sided choice of documents from texts and representations of the official theology.[2] Posener took as his basic material the literary texts and proved in a convincing argument that the common people really looked upon the king primarily as a human being. They considered him to have a divine character only when he performed official ceremonies. That is, the institution of pharaoh might be divine, but the king himself was divine only for certain purposes and certain situations, and only while he was alive. Accordingly, we have no right to assume that the Egyptians accorded each king overall divinity.

Of course, a pharaoh might be venerated after his death, at first as an extension of the funerary cult, and, like Imhotep and Amenhotep, he might eventually be elevated, individually, to the rank of a saint or a god. This the Egyptians did in the case of Djoser and Snofru, and Mentuhotep or Amenhotep I, who founded the classical periods of ancient Egypt, the Old, Middle, and New Kingdom.[3]

In actuality, it turns out that divine kingship was limited to a king after he had died, or to a king while he was alive only during the time of his official performances. The rest of the time he was considered to be a human being, surely not an ordinary one, but never a god. Naturally, the kings realized this all too clearly themselves, as is indicated by the endeavors of many of them to persuade the Egyptian citizen to transfer the specific divine character of the institution to the person of the king. The pharaoh tried to convince his subjects of his superhuman nature, to invite his people to venerate him as an intermediary, a saint, and to present himself as something he was not: a personal god. For example, the king might have texts produced to convey his divinity and various representations made of himself on monuments or statues that included a divine iconography. Thus, from the earliest times the kings wore the nemes headdress; or various crowns. But from the time of the Eighteenth Dynasty some had themselves portrayed wearing the horn of a ram winding around the ear. This was the symbol of Amun, the emblem of the god given to him by his followers in Nubia and the Sudan during the Middle Kingdom.[4] The king hoped that the association would reflect on him as well. Thus, the Egyptians portrayed Tuthmosis III and Amenhotep II wearing the ram's horn in the tombs of User-Amun and Ken-Amun.[5] Likewise, Tuthmosis IV can be seen, in Cairo, represented as a giffin on his war chariot with the ram's horn, trampling his enemies.[6] Since late prehistoric times, the griffin was regarded as

Fig. 2. Chariot of Thutmosis IV. The king as a griffon with the ram's horn

Fig. 3. Coronation of Amenhotep III at Luxor. The ram's horn at the crown

Fig. 4. Amenhotep III in his temple at Soleb as a god venerated by himself

Fig. 5. Sethos I in his temple at Abydos, wearing the Blue Crown and the ram's horn

a divine animal, and the griffin, the ram's horn, and the chariot convey the propaganda—the king shows himself to his enemies to be the godlike lord of his country. Then the Egyptians portray Amenhotep III in a relief in the Luxor Temple receiving the horn of Amun during his coronation.[7] And in the temple of Soleb he may be seen making an offering in his normal royal costume to himself, deified with the horn and the sun disk and crescent.[8] In the Ramesside Period Sethos I is portrayed with the ram's horn on the processional way to his cult chapel in the main temple, and in the king's chapel of the Osiris complex at Abydos.[9] And Sethos had himself presented in this temple as well, in order to convey the idea that he, as an Osiris, was divine. Even Osiris is equipped with the horn![10] Later, Ramses II was portrayed in his temple in Abydos sitting in the boat of the sun god, drawn by the souls of Pe and Nekhen.[11] He is trying to show himself as an earthy manifestation of the sun god and, of course, he wears the ram's horn around his ear. He wears the horn again in the small Temple in the first court of the Luxor temple serving with Amun (who is shown only as his sacred symbol, no doubt to emphasize the divinity of the king even more).[12] Ramses II is presented no less than six times in his temple at Abu Simbel appearing as a god, with the horn, always adored by his human personality.[13] He also is shown in the sun temple of Abu Simbel receiving the horn during his coronation by Toth and Harakhte.[14] The Egyptians again show Ramses with the horn, sharing the divine mastery of the small temple of Hathor and Nefertari, with Nefertari.[15] Finally, the kings of Kushite and Meroitic times continued to use the symbol of Amun to emphasize their sacral character even more than the Egyptian kings did.[16]

It is clear that the kings of Egypt did not feel that their "normal" outfit was sufficient to win them a divinity that would raise them to the level of "great" gods. They felt that they needed special symbols in order that they might assume this rank, and one way they tried to do this, as we have seen, was to wear the ram's horn of Amun. But, as I briefly mentioned above, the kings also tried to achieve acceptance as being godlike by associating themselves with the sun god. Thus, they had themselves portrayed with the sun disk above their heads. The kings of the Fifth Dynasty began to try to relate themselves to the sun god and continued to do so into the time of the New Kingdom by using the sun disk as the equivalent of a crown.[17]

Many of the kings of Egypt also constructed colossi to convey their superhuman qualities to the people, rather than their individual

Fig. 6. Ramses II in his temple at Abydos, wearing the ram's horn and
identified with the sun god

Fig. 7. Ramses II and his wife as divine lords of the small temple of
Abu Simbel

Fig. 8. The ram's horn in the meroitic royal costume. Meroe Pyramid
N. 6

Fig. 9. Colossus of Ramses II at Luxor, bearing its proper name on the shoulder

characteristics. The kings also were careful to place their statues strategically, as at the boundaries of the sacred and profane areas, or at the gate or in the forecourt of the temples, to impress the worshippers and to indicate that they were divine intermediaries between the people and the gods. And the kings encouraged veneration of their royal colossi, and themselves, by erecting stelae close by that were carved with invocations addressed to themselves.[18] Often the kings represented themselves in their huge statues as the standard bearer of the sacred emblem of the principle god of a sanctuary, dressed in a panther skin, and coming out of the inner temple as the only legitimate priest. In this way the kings hoped to express their divinity, as intermediaries between man and god.

The kings also resorted to the so-called Osiris pillars to convey their divinity, first in the lower temple of the Bent Pyramid at Dahshur.[19] We can see the political "earthly" king striding up to his own figure coming out of the wall. The king's close connection with the wall and the pillars indicates his close relationship to the stone and the earth. He is divine as is Osiris, because both come from the earth. Normally, the kings were represented wearing a special royal apron with a pendant, as at Abu Simbel, Gerf Hussein, Medinet Habu, and Karnak, that were carved during the Ramesside Period. But already, during the Middle Kingdom they are portrayed wearing the garment of Osiris and the afnet headdress while they come out of the niche, or stand or sit in it.[20]

The kings of Egypt also attempted to proclaim their divinity by having themselves portrayed in close contact with the gods (this subject matter is not used in private sculpture until the Late Period).[21] At first, during the time of the Old Kingdom, the king is shown with the god's hand resting on his head.[22] Or, he is shown as the living Horus being suckled by his divine mother Isis (the Egyptians often linked the mother-child relationship with theology).[23] This is, perhaps, the significance of the famous group statue showing Pepi II with his mother.[24] Gradually, the Egyptians began to show the king standing alone with the gods. He has become one of them. The king often appears in a triad, but not in the context of a holy family of father, mother, and son (the king would be the son in this case). He is present to express the fact that the totality of the gods, symbolized by the trinity, would be incomplete without the king and that the king's claim to divinity cannot be confirmed without his entering the trinity. There are some especially good examples of these group figures at Abu Simbel. At first, the king was not yet recognized as an associate of

Fig. 10. Standard bearer of Ramses
II at ancient Memphis

Fig. 11. Niche statue of the Middle Kingdom at Abydos

Fig. 12. Head of a coronation group, probably Tutanckamun

the gods, but, when he finally became such, he merely added his figure to those of the gods already in place.[25] Later, after the king had promoted himself as a deity, he included himself in the reliefs as they were carved, which was done at Abu Simbel in the late reliefs and in the temple of Wadi es-Sebua.[26]

It is important to note that the examples of the triad, god-king-god, are concentrated in the eastern delta, especially in Tanis, and in Nubia, besides Abu Simbel, at Gerf Hussein and Kasr Ibrim.[27] Apparently, the Egyptians who lived in Egypt were not so ready to accept the equivalence of the king with the gods, but those who lived at the edges of the empire were more willing to do so. And this was fortunate because it was very important to convince these people in particular of the power and importance of the Egyptian kingship, the king being so far removed physically from them.

Some of the kings tried to convey the fact that they had superhu-

16

Fig. 13. Pepi II and his mother

Fig. 14. Triad of Haremhab (?)

man characteristics by having themselves represented as sacred animals. In late prehistoric and protodynastic times the bull, lion, dog, and falcon were generally accepted as symbols of the king and kingship, but not of any divine qualities the king might want to convey. In historical times, the Egyptians had come to use these animals to express the special divinity of the king. Snefru, who was in many respects the prototype of the divine king, was represented as a falcon, for instance, in Sinai.[28] Several kings of the New Kingdom incorporate signs of the sacred bird Horus into their costumes. Ramses II is

18

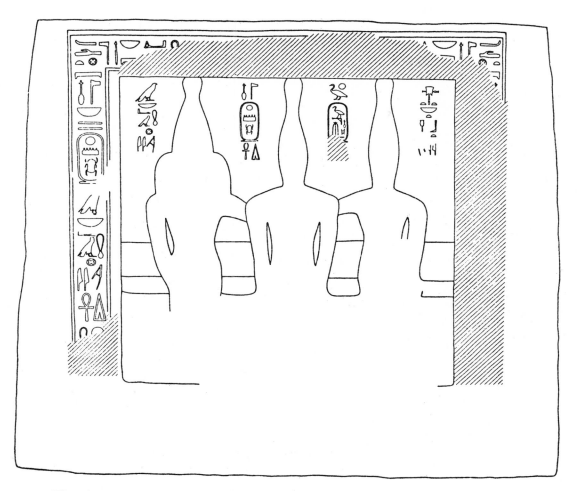

Fig. 15. Statue group at Kasr Ibrim. King embraced by the gods

signified with a falcon's head;[29] Nektanebis is a falcon in his sanctuary in Saqqâra.[30] Many kings were memorialized as a sphinx, which was neither human nor animal. However, the sphinx was neither pure god nor pure king either, and the ancient Egyptian could more readily understand the king to be both a god and a king if he were represented as a sphinx. The most famous example of the ambiguous sphinx, of course, is at Gîza.[31] It was originally made as a colossal, and therefore divine, statue of a king, but later the Egyptians came to regard it as a representation of the god Harakhte. And the fact that the sphinx was so ambiguous a symbol also encouraged the foreign workers in Memphis to see in it their god, Hurun. The sphinx was perhaps not a very definitive symbol for a king to rely upon to convey an image of his divinity as a great god.

19

Fig. 16. Ramses II added to a community of gods. Abu Simbel, great temple

Once the king established that he had become deified through any of the means described above, he could arrange to provide himself with a temple and a processional barge. These barges of deified kings can be seen everywhere in the Nubian temples of Ramses II, for example.[32] And "Amenhotep in the ship" and "Ramses in the ship" become accepted names for deified manifestations of these kings. The temples were cut into the solid rock of the cliffs and called *speos*. They were evolved from rock chapels in which the goddess Hathor was worshipped as the mother of the reigning king. The chapel was originally considered to be the place where the young king was suckled by a goddess and then was transferred into the place where the king himself had become a god.[33] In the Eighteenth Dynasty, several

Fig. 17.   The Sphinx of Giza

Fig. 18. The seven gods in the Sanctuary of Haremhab's temple at Silsila

Fig. 19. Veneration of the king's name. Graffito on Sehel Island

22

Fig. 20. Anagraphic names of Ramses
II. Great temple of Abu Simbel

of these rock temples were carved at Qasr Ibrim in Nubia, in which
the king sits between the gods to form the triad and acts as one of the
gods of the chapel. The Egyptians carved other rock temples like this
at Ellesiya, at Silsila, in the Wadi Mia for Sethos I, and six temples for
Ramses II at Elkab, Beit el-Wali, Gerf Hussein, Wadi es-Sebua, ed-
Derr, and Abu Simbel.[34] The groups of statues carved in these temples are a more imposing version of the niche figures and Osiris
figures which I have already discussed.[35]

The kings began to reinforce the fact that they were truly divine by
adding cartouches to their statues and reliefs, which make their name
the bearer of a certain divinity, as well as indicating their place in
politics and history.[36] Originally their cartouches had a purely
theological meaning; they were used to associate the king with the sun
god and to express the religious function of the kings as intermediaries between god and man. This was the case when they were
put on the bow or the gold hieroglyph and surmounted by a pair of
feathers or often the sun disk to be venerated by private persons.
Many of these are to be found in regions near the border of Egypt, at
any place where the king must act as the only representative of order
and welfare in the midst of hostile, dangerous, and inhospitable surroundings.

The cartouches gradually came to be considered as symbols to de-

Fig. 21. Name statue of Ramses II

Fig. 22. "Anat of Ramses" on a relief

scribe the political activities of the kings, and the Egyptians felt that they had to drop them from a king's name when they wished to describe a godlike activity.[37] In addition, when the Egyptians wanted to emphasize some superhuman quality that was part of the name of a king, they presented all the hieroglyphs of his name but enlarged those which depicted the names of any gods, so that they dominated the other signs in the name.[38]

Thus, on the one hand, the enlarged hieroglyphs symbolize the direct influence of the gods on everyone and everything, including the relationship of the god with the king himself, and, on the other, the hieroglyphs call special dogmatic attention to the divinity of the king. The enlarged hieroglyphs in the names, which we may call "anagraphic names," were isolated from the context of the royal titles and the Egyptians made independent pictures out of them or even three-dimensional representations of the kind. Such are the famous headdress from Bubastis, the name statue of Ramses II in Cairo, or the anagram of the same king above the doorway of the great temple at Abu Simbel.[39]

Kings often added epithets after their names, which the Egyptians

Fig. 23. Statue of Ramses II venerated by Ramses as a living king

considered to be among the criteria the individual must meet to warrant divine worship (political titles were placed before the name).[40] Some of these simply describe the king's acceptance by a god: "Ramses beloved of Atum" (which later was transformed into "Ramses who is venerated as Atum"; the king has progressed from the role of interpreter between man and god to the earthly representative of the god).[41] The Egyptians used these epithets, describing the divine character of some aspect of the king until the Saitic period, on the colossi, standard bearers, and statue groups I have already described, to convey the divinity of their kings. And, as I have pointed out above, concerning the other religious symbols, the epithets establish the king as the earthly representative of a god, sometimes even a new god created for the first time with a rather limited following; they also are used to transform the political power of the god to religious importance.[42] And gradually the idea that the anagraphic names convey, i.e., of a king accepted by a god, was transformed to the point that the king selects some god to become his divine manifestation. Thus, the well-known "Ramses whom Re has loved/elected" becomes "Re whom Ramses has loved/elected."[43] Consequently, we can identify Anat when she is described as "Anat of Ramses" as a divine form of Ramses himself in the shape of the goddess.[44]

After a king has managed to convey himself to the people as a god by using all of the means we have described, we still must examine the divine form that he really takes. He never can become a true divinity. That is, no king can take over the existing shape or character of any Egyptian god to show and prove his own divinity. This would be really extraordinary because the Egyptians held steadfastly to the fact that the position of an Egyptian god cannot be occupied by a mortal, and this holds for a mortal king as well. Thus, the kings must contrive original entities outside of the pantheon by which to associate themselves with the gods, and we can thereby see that the nature of the kings will never be the same as the nature of the gods, and that the king's divinity will be of an inferior quality to that of the gods'. This is true, for one reason, because the great gods of the pantheon have unlimited roles to fulfill which give them the possibilities of being free *and eternal* in the exercise of their activities. The kings must create deities of local character and limited duration. That is, the divine forms of the kings are limited in space, time, and content. They are ephemeral gods, and the maximum duration of their effectiveness is the lifetime of the monarch.

Despite the fact that the minor divine kings were inferior to the great gods of the pantheon, and were limited in their influence, they were much more appealing to the common people than the distant, impersonal gods. That is, the people could see the king participating in the human as well as the divine world, and his superhuman nature could also be presented in comprehensible images, as, for example, in the colossi in front of the temples or in a relief showing the king smiting an enemy.[45] The king, as a god, filled a vacuum in the religious life of the common people which was brought about when the gods of old were further and further removed from them as the system of the theology became more complicated. Nevertheless, the people never worshipped the complete personality of any king; they only appreciated one or several of the aspects or strengths of his character. This reserve, this refusal of the simple man to venerate the reigning king as a god shows us, more than anything else, the basis for the limitations that were imposed on the divinity of the pharaoh. As long as he lived, and no matter what he did, no king of Egypt was able to ascend to the realm of the great gods.

Two mortals did, as we shall see.

NOTES

1. *Le régime pharaonique,* 2 vols. (1912–1913); *Du caractère religieux de la royauté pharaonique* (1902).
2. With an excellent account of the development of the question on pp. VII–XV. For some new aspects of the question see D. Wildung in *OLZ* 68 (1973), 549–565.
3. See D. Wildung, *Die Rolle ägyptischer Könige im Bewusstsein ihrer Nachwelt* (1969), 58–93 (Djoser), 105–152 (Snefru), L. Habachi, *MDAIK* 19 (1963), 16–52; until the urgently necessary reexamination of all documents, see J. Cerný, *BIFAO* 27 (1927), 159–203.
4. E.g. Boston MFA 20.1180: G. A. Reisner, *Kerma* IV–V (1923), pl. 37.
5. TT 131: *PM* I², 246 (8); TT 93: *PM* I², 191 (9).
6. H. Carter—P. E. Newberry, *The Tomb of Thoutmôsis* IV (1904), 31, pl. 12.
7. *PM* II², 320 (122); K. Michalowski, *Luxor* (1972), pl. 49.
8. *LD* III, 84c, 85a, 87b, 87c.
9. A. Calverley, *The Temple of King Sethos I at Abydos* III (1938), pl. 35, 38, 40., and *o.c.,* IV (1958), pl. 44.
10. Berlin 20134/5: R. Anthes *MDAIK* 12 (1943), pl. 10–11.
11. *PM* VI, 36 (31)–(32).
12. *PM* II², 310 (41)–(42).
13. *PM* VII, 104 (43), (44), 106 (48), 108

(84), 109 (94), (97); see L. Habachi, *Features of the Deification of Ramesses II* (1969), pl. 2a, 3, 4a, b.

14. *PM* VII, 99 (22).

15. Scene C 14: Chr. Desroches Noblecourt—Ch. Kuentz, *Le petit temple d' Abou Simbel* (1968), pl. 55–56; scene M6: *ibid.*, pl. 121–122.

16. E.g. J. Leclant, *Monuments thébains de la XXVe dynastie* (1965), pl. 69 B; *LD* V, 2a, 10; e.g. *LD* V, 40, 41, 56, 64, 66; see I. Hofmann, *Studien zum meroitischen Königtum* (1971), 46–47, 49, 53.

17. Sahure: Cairo 28/2/21/17; see D. Wildung, *ZÄS* 99 (1972), 33–41.

18. E.g. the large complex of the so-called Horbeit-Stelae from Pi-Ramesse: L. Habachi, *ASAE* 52 (1954), 501–559. R. Khawam, *BIFAO* 70 (1971), 137–146, pl. 32.

19. A. Fakhry, *The Monuments of Sneferu at Dahshur* II/1 (1961), 111 ff., fig. 119, 120, 127.

20. E.g. Cairo: H. G. Evers, *Staat aus dem Stein* I (1929), 111, fig. 27; Copenhague AEIN 1482: O. Koefoed-Petersen, *Catalogue des statues et statuettes égyptiennes* (1950), 16, pl. 22; unpublished niche-statue in the 2nd court of the temple of Sethos I at Abydos.

21. E.g. the statue-groups of Mycerinus: W. Wood, *JEA* 60 (1974), 82–93.

22. Coronation groups, see W. K. Simpson, *JEA* 41 (1955), 122–114.

23. P. Lacau and H. Chevrier, *Une chappelle de Sésostris Ier,: Planches* (1969), pl. 12, 37; e.g. G. Jéquier, *Le monument funéraire de Pépi II,* II (1938), pl. 30, 32.

24. Brooklyn 39.119: *Brief Guide to the Department of Ancient Art* (1970), 30–31.

25. *PM* VII, 104 (43), (44), 109 (94), (97); L. Habachi, *Features of the Deification of Ramesses II* (1969), pl. 3, 4.

26. E.g. *PM* VII, 109 (100) ff.; *PM* VII, 60 (69), (72), (76), (84), 61 (88), (91), (97)–(99); L. Habachi, *o.c.*, pl. 7a.

27. E.g. P. Montet, *Nouvelles fouilles de Tanis* (1933), pl. 24–25, 54–55, 59–60, 70. *PM* VII, 34–35 (9)–(10), (13)–(14); *LD* III, 178a, b. R. A. Caminos, *The Shrines and Rock-Inscriptions of Ibrim* (1968).

28. Brit. Mus. 41745: *PM* VII, 358; D. Wildung, *Die Rolle ägyptischer Könige im Bewusstsein ihrer Nachwelt* (1969), 111–113.

29. Abu Simbel: *LD* III, 189c; L. Habachi, *o.c.*, 6, pl. 1a.

30. J. Yoyotte, *Kêmi* 15 (1959), 70–74; H. De Meulenaere, *CdE* 69/35 (1960), 92–107.

31. For the documentation, see S. Hassan, *The Great Sphinx and Its Secrets* (=*Excavations at Giza VIII*) (1953).

32. E.g. L. Habachi, *o.c.*, 6, 13–15, pl. 6.

33. The most ancient *speos* is the Hathor Cave in Serabit el-Khadim (twelfth dynasty), followed by the Speos Artemidos of Hatshepsut. *PM* II², 380–381. Perhaps there was a rock chapel of Hathor at Deir el-Bahari already in the eleventh dynasty.

34. R. A. Caminos, *The Shrines and Rock-Inscriptions of Ibrim* (1969); Chr. Desroches-Noblecourt, S. Donadoni, and G. Moukhtar, *Le spéos d'el-Lessiya* I (1968), 19–20, pl. 26, 36–38; *PM* V, 213 (60); S. Schott, *Kanais—Der Tempel Sethos I. im Wadi Mia* (1961), pl. 9; Ph. Derchain, *Elkab I* (1971), 6–7, pl. 16a; *PM* VII, 27 (43); *PM* VII, 36 (40); *PM* VII, 62 (122); *PM* VII, 89 (29); *PM* VII, 110 (115).

35. *PM* IV, 17 (lower).

36. See A. Radwan, *SAK* 2 (1975) (in the press).

37. E.g., in most of the references from Abu Simbel given above, n. 215–216.

38. See D. Wildung, *OLZ* 68 (1973), 556–557.

39. E. Naville, *Bubastis* (1891), 34–35, pl. 21; Cairo JE 64735: J. Vandier, *Manuel d'archéologie égyptienne* III, pl. 133, 2; *PM* VII, 101 (upper); L. Habachi, *Features of the Deification of Ramesses II* (1969), 9–10, fig. 8, pl. 5a.

40. J. Yoyotte in *Akten des 24. Internationalen Orientalisten-Kongresses München 1957* (1959), 54–56.

41. See E. Otto, *MDAIK* 25 (1969), 98–100.

42. For a general account see L. Habachi, *o.c.*

43. G. Daressy, *ASAE* 4 (1903), 282.

44. Brooklyn 54.67: J. D. Cooney, *Five Years of Collecting Egyptian Art* (1956), 27–28, pl. 51–52. *PM* II², 313 (70), (71); L. Habachi, *o.c.*, 18–20, fig. 13, pl. 9a, 11. GL 88. *Catalogue* (1972), 61.

45. E.g. the so-called Horbeit-Stelae; see n. 203 above; a group of stelae from Memphis: W. M. F. Petrie, *Memphis* I (1909), pl. 7–8; similarly at Deir el-Medineh: B. Bruyère, *Rapport Deir el-Médineh* (1935–1940) II (1952), pl. 38.

30

CHAPTER TWO

Imhotep

Occasionally, "ordinary" humans of extraordinary powers, came to be venerated by the people. Through the example of their own success, which they gained from their personal effort, they came to be considered as the ideal mediators between man and king and man and god. And so they were surrounded by the myth of a man of genius and mystery as being a favorite of the gods.[1] Most of these "saints" never were accepted into the pantheon; as I have indicated, they were venerated only for a brief period of time.[2] But this is not the case with the person whom everybody usually remembers immediately when one speaks of the deification of private people in Egypt. I refer, of course, to Imhotep. He was the author of wisdom literature, a famous physician, an architect who built the Step Pyramid of King Djoser, and a counsellor of his king. Imhotep was the greatest of the intellects of the first great period in the early Old Kingdom.[3] And perhaps he is the first individual personality we know at all.[4]

The only monument of Imhotep dating from his lifetime that attests to the greatness which the Egyptians ascribed to him is the standing figure of King Djoser in the Cairo Museum.[5] On the left of the front side of the base is carved the short inscription:

Fig. 24. Statue base from Saqqâra with Imhotep's signature

The seal-bearer of the King of Lower Egypt, **ḥrj-tp-njsw.t,** ruler of the great house, **irj-p ^c.t,** the high priest of Heliopolis, Imhotep [is] the chief of the sculptors, of the masons and of the producers of stone-vessels.

The titles preceding his name indicate that Imhotep performed the highest functions in the administration and in the cult of the sun-god Re. The nomina following his name indicate that Imhotep was the architect of the Step Pyramid; at least he was described as the supervisor of all the work done in a great building project. (The fact that the statue originally was placed in a small statue room on the south side of the entrance colonnade of the enclosure around the pyramid seems to corroborate this).

The greatness of Imhotep is perhaps further indicated from the titles, now including that of chief lector-priest, to be found on inscribed stone vessels in the basements of the Step Pyramid.[6] Although his name was not inscribed along with the titles, they probably refer to

Fig. 25. Step Pyramid of King Djoser, built by Imhotep

him; it is unlikely that these high ranks would be held by two individuals at the same time.

Imhotep may well have begun his career as an architect during the reign of Chasechemui, when stone was first used as a building material on a considerable scale. (This king constructed a sanctuary at Hieraconpolis partly of red granite[7] and a stone tomb in Abydos.) After Chasechemui died, about 2635 B.C., Imhotep completed his apprenticeship during the reign of Nebka, the successor to Chasechemui and founder of the Third Dynasty. (This is indicated by a small inscription on the Palermo Stone, the annals of the Old Kingdom, where we read about the building of some stone structures in the reign of this king.[8]) Imhotep then continued his work for King Djoser, during which time he mastered his craft. Nor did he stop after Djoser died, about 2600 B.C. We find his name in a graffito on the enclosure wall of the Unfinished Pyramid, started during the reign of Horus Skhemkhet, who succeded King Djoser.[9] (The continuity of architectural development in the Third Dynasty is thus explained by the identity of the architect.)

Many have assumed that an individual as important as Imhotep was indicated to be would have had a tomb not far from the king's

33

own tomb. And the notion that Imhotep was buried in Saqqâra near the king has been carried down through the ages, by the Arab writers of the Middle Ages, and ultimately by Kurt Sethe in 1902.[10] Accordingly, excavators have tried to find the tomb, but with no success. Walter B. Emery might possibly have discovered the site, in the mastaba 3518.[11] It can be dated to the time of Djoser by the location and clay seals. Also, Emery found anatomical donaria and votive vessels at the entrance that are typical of worship. But any exact proof whereby we can assign the tomb remains missing. The question remains open and we shall have to wait.

We have no clear records that Imhotep was remembered, much less venerated, for the thousand years after his death until the beginning of the New Kingdom, when his name appears once again. (But the Egyptians did begin to worship him again, and for this reason he must have been held in some regard during the interim period from which we have so far found nothing.) We do have a rather unimportant reminiscence of him dating from the Sixth Dynasty. He possibly was memorialized in the place name "Doorway of Ij-hotep" referred to by a man named Uni as a collecting point in Memphis for some military expeditions that Uni conducted for King Pepi I.[12] His name seems to have been mentioned in the Papyrus Westcar, even if it is destroyed in the original text.[13] Nevertheless, in the first of four fairy tales in this papyrus, the name of King Djoser is given and a reference is made to a "first lector-priest," which, of course, also appears on the stone vessels from Saqqâra.[14] As in the case of the vessels, the title here also very likely could refer to Imhotep.

Finally, in a Theban tomb of the time of Amenhotep III we find the following text addressed to the owner of the tomb:

> The *wab*-priest may give offerings to your *ka*. The *wab*-priests may stretch to you their arms with libations on the soil, as it is done for Imhotep with the remains of the water bowl.[15]

Imhotep apparently was offered this libation regularly, as is confirmed by the invocation that is frequently written on the papyrus roll included on the statues of Imhotep dating up to the Late Period:

> Water from the water-pot of every scribe for your *ka*, O Imhotep.[16]

Over the course of the centuries Imhotep had evolved from his image as an intellectual to become the patron of intellectuals, and then the patron of the scribes. His role as patron of the intellectual arts found its expression in a fixed ritual, which indicated that it had become sanctioned by the cult.

But it was not simply the vague memory of a great man of the past which caused the Egyptians to deify Imhotep. His following also rested on the intellectual qualities, experience, and the wisdom he expressed in some literary works he was said to have composed, as is mentioned, for example, in the *Harper's Song*.[17] "I have heard the sayings of Imhotep and Hordjedef, which we quoted in proverbs so much."

This indicates that the literary works of Imhotep were as well known as those of Hordjedef (who *was* well known to the Egyptians as a sage who served Djoser and the son of Cheops respectively as well as a writer of wisdom teachings.)[18]

Imhotep's fame as a writer is further substantiated in the early Ramesside papyrus, Chester Beatty IV, as well as on a relief from a private tomb in Saqqâra. In the text of the papyrus he and Hordjedef are hailed as being among many scribes who became immortal through their writing:

Is there any here like Hordjedef? Is there another like Imhotep? There have been none among our kindred like Neferti and Cheti, that chief among them. I recall to you the names of Ptah-em-Djehuti and Chacheperreseneb. Is there another one like Ptahhotep or like Kairsu?[19]

In this group of immortals, whose original works are almost all preserved, Imhotep finds his place. On the tomb relief at Saqqâra, the Egyptians included the name of Imhotep with other famous scribes in a long list of different groups of people of renown in ancient times, including kings, viziers, high priests of Memphis, and chief embalmers.[20]

The Egyptians living during the time of the New Kingdom apparently continued to revere the name of Imhotep. This might be substantiated from a statement on an unplaced fragment from the Royal Canon of Turin:

. . . The son of Ptah, born by the lady . . . who gives life. . . .[21]

Such a passage indicates that Imhotep must have been held in high

Fig. 26. *Harper's Song* in the tomb of Pa-iten-em-heb, mentioning
Imhotep

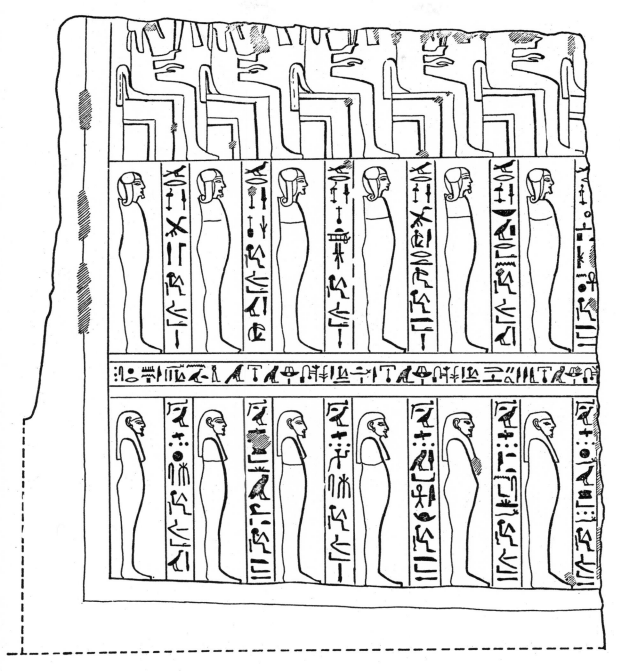

Fig. 27. Part of a tomb wall at Saqqâra with a list of famous people of
Egypt's past

regard, for his name is listed in a text which otherwise records nothing but the names and dates of the kings of Egypt. Further, the Egyptians must have included him again when, after the name of King Huni, who ruled at the end of the Third Dynasty, we read:

> . . . The architect, who conducts. . . .[22]

This surely cannot be a remark referring to the king himself. Thus, the Egyptians must have thought as highly of Imhotep as they did of their kings to have placed his name in the Turin Papyrus.

It might be tempting to combine the text from the two fragments of the Canon, seemingly so out of place with the rest of the papyrus, to indicate further that Imhotep was held to be as venerable as the kings and to be put in their company.

> The king of Upper and Lower Egypt, Huni; 24 years. During his reign died in the architect who conducts. . . . Imhotep, the son of Ptah, borne by the lady Khereduankh, who gives life to the people. . . .

The fact that King Huni ruled during the Third Dynasty, when Imhotep was active, the reference to an architect (who most likely would not be a king but when Imhotep was an architect), the epithet "son of Ptah," which became a stereotyped part of his name after the Late Period, all make us think of Imhotep. Of course, this reconstruction cannot be substantiated by any means now at hand. However, we can refer to Manetho's report on the Third Dynasty, which is almost a translation of the text in Turin, for some substantiation:

> . . . and he was the inventor of the art of building with hewn stone. He also devoted attention to writing.[23]

It does not matter that Manetho ascribes these achievements, not to Imhotep himself, but to King Djoser, who is the personification of all achievements (and takes the credit for them) during his reign.

Documents dating from the New Kingdom establish that Imhotep had become the patron of the scribes and that he was the offspring of a god. As I have indicated, the scribes had developed a cult for Imhotep by that time, and before the time of the Twenty-sixth Dynasty his renown had become so great that he was accorded a sanctuary at Saqqâra. Perhaps the installation of a cult for Imhotep was brought about by the family of a man named Iahmes and his ancestors. A Memphite priest of the Persian Period, he is called on his statue (formerly in Berlin):

Priest of Imhotep, Son-of-Ptah[24]

And his great-great-grandfather, who lived in the time of Psammetich II was

Servant of the gods of the Temple of Imhotep, Son-of-Ptah.

The family also was employed by the ancient kings Djoser and Djoser-Teti, both closely linked to Imhotep, as we have seen. They apparently constructed a temple to Imhotep in the Twenty-sixth Dynasty, and the location can be established from the numerous titles of Iahmes. It was built in an area called "the mountain," which corresponds to an area in north Saqqâra which rises as a hill from the surrounding plains.

However, the deification of Imhotep remained localized around the area of Memphis. Khenemibrê, chief architect, mentions him in an inscription in the Wadi Hammâmâb in the year 36 of Darius, where he puts at the top of his geneology:

. . . chief architect of Upper and Lower Egypt, mayor and vizier Rahotep, whose renown is equal to that of the chief architect of Upper and Lower Egypt, mayor, vizier and chief lector-priest of the king of Upper and Lower Egypt, Djoser, Imhotep.[25]

But even at this late date, there is still no mention of superhuman or even divine qualities of Imhotep as there were at Saqqâra.

Nevertheless, from this time on, Imhotep became more and more generally regarded as a god, as is attested to by the fact that a great number of figures have been found dating from the Twenty-sixth or Twenty-seventh Dynasty onwards. One of the most ancient examples is a basalt statue in the Louvre dedicated by a man named Wahibrê.[26] The characteristics of the iconography of Imhotep are already developed in this figure: a sitting posture (otherwise very rare in the Late Period), the long apron, the tight cap, and the papyrus unrolled on his lap. The papyrus bears the votive offering:

Fig. 28. Statue of Imhotep

Fig. 29. Bronze figure of Imhotep

Fig. 29. Bronze figure of Imhotep

Water from the water-pot of every scribe to your *ka*, O Imhotep.

This image of the reading man was regarded by the Egyptians as a symbol of wisdom, of a contact to the past through the knowledge of literature, as a symbol of divine inspiration which has its influence upon man through the person represented by the statue. In detail, the long apron symbolized the priest, the papyrus was the symbol of the wise man or writer, and the cap was the sign of Ptah, Imhotep's divine father. The iconography of Imhotep remained essentially unchanged in all of the images the Egyptians made through the Late and Ptolemaic Periods.

Almost 400 bronze statuettes are known of Imhotep (most are from Saqqâra and Memphis), which indicates that he enjoyed a vigorous cult. On many of these statues, he is no longer called by his simple name but by his divine name, Imhotep, Son-of-Ptah. He is now a member of the pantheon in Memphis. In addition to these votive figures, Egyptians also made statues of dedicators presenting an image of the god to his sanctuary,[27] further substantiating the popularity that the cult of Imhotep had attained.

By the time of the Thirtieth Dynasty, the Egyptians had come to regard Imhotep as one of the important dieties of Memphis. In a relief made from Saqqâra, during the Thirtieth Dynasty and now in Marseille, a donor is depicted worshipping the triad Apis-Osiris, Imhotep, and Ptah.[24] Imhotep, Son-of-Ptah is now shown wearing the sign of life and bearing a composite scepter (in addition to his usual costume), both divine prerogatives. The inscription calls him

August god, who gives life to the people.

The bottom lines contain the statement

Praise to Apis-Osiris and to all these who are behind Apis, to all the messengers of this hall at this doorway.

Besides Ptah, the divine chief, and Apis, the incarnated god, Imhotep has become the third member of the community of gods.

Imhotep has appropriated the attributes of giving life to the people, acting as a healer, and serving as the messenger for "this door," a reference to a chapel near the entrance to the Serapeum. He is venerated at the door of the temple, at the border of the profane

Fig. 30. Worship of Imhotep at Saqqâra

and the holy, between which he mediates. During the Thirtieth
Dynasty Imhotep had become known as a healer, as well as an architect and a man of wisdom, as is indicated in the relief from Marseille. His role as a healer is further indicated on the statue of Psentais
in the Vatican.[29] The inscription on this statue dedicated to Imhotep,
mentions him as the only god in the offering:

> An offering which the king gives [to] Imhotep, Son-of-Ptah, who
> comes to everybody imploring him, who heals illness, who cures
> the members.

Here, Imhotep acts as helper, with the special character of a healer.
Again, his role as a healer is indicated on a statue offered by Psentaes,
who makes an offering of thanks for being cured in the sanctuary of
Imhotep in Saqqâra. (The fact that Psentais was a pilgrim indicates
that the celebrity of Imhotep was already widespread and attracting
people from other towns.)

The Egyptians also prayed to him to provide children and wives

44

Fig. 31. Statue dedicated to Imhotep

. . . who came from the nomes and towns to pray for life to the master of life, that he may give a son to everybody begging for it, a wife to everybody imploring it, and that he may heal all suffering children.

However, these responsibilities are not so much typical of Imhotep himself. It is the duty of any popular diety to solve the problems of health and the problems of the family.

Thus, during the Thirtieth Dynasty the cult of Imhotep was highly regarded. We have a torso from the time of this dynasty, now in the Brooklyn Museum,[30] on which an inscription has been carved that is similar to that on the statue dedicated by Psentaes:

. . . who came from towns and nomes to implore for life to the august god, who gives life to the people, to Imhotep, Son-of-Ptah.

The titles show that the donor was a learned man with special knowledge in literature, medicine, and oracular practices, knowledge typical of the chief lector-priest and magician, and all touching the field of activities of Imhotep.

By the end of the Thirtieth Dynasty the reigning kings had fully acknowledged the cult of Imhotep. Nectanebo II called himself "beloved of Imhotep, Son-of-Ptah."[31] The high standing of the cult is indicated, as well, by the fine quality of the statues given by the worshippers of Imhotep and by the high social position of the donors. Pieces of poor quality and wholesale ware are unknown; the cult of Imhotep had become a noble cult, a matter of the upper classes.

As I mentioned above, old sources indicate that the Temple of Imhotep was probably located in the north Saqqâra, although the temple has never been found. Ptolemaic documents, demotic, and Greek papyri from Memphis[32] and a stela from north Saqqâra[33] give more details about the temple, as well as a description of the people who served the deity. The temple is described as having a forecourt and a dromos and included a domain extending to the boundary of the cultivated fields. Besides the temple, these sources mention a quarter in Memphis called the "Town of Imhotep" which was situated southwest of the temple of Ptah. The temple itself was served by priests, temple scribes, scribes of Imhotep in every second and fourth group of priests, royal scribes for all the taxes in the house of Imhotep, and embalmers. The Egyptians had placed Imhotep in the community of the great gods of Memphis, as is described on the stela;[34] he is mentioned with Osiris (Osiris-Apis), Isis, the mother of Apis, Harendotes, Thoth the thrice great, Anubis, and the ram of Mendes. The Egyptians made no difference in the divinity of any of these gods; accordingly, Imhotep's priests served these gods as well. (It is interesting to note that each of the gods mentioned above had an animal cemetery associated with him: to Osiris, the Serapeum; to Isis, the cow galleries or Iseum, to Harendotes, the falcon catacombs; to Thoth, the ibis and baboon galleries, to Anubis, the dog catacombs; and to the ram of Mendes, a ram cemetery. On the animal mummies found in these places, we also find the figure of Imhotep.)[35]

The ritual that had been established to worship Imhotep appears to have involved making a libation in large vessels which were made in the shape of the typical form of the scribes' water pot. The simple people continued to worship him, and in the Ptolemaic Period he became even more popular to the extent that the free access of all to "the door" was eventually guaranteed in a legal text.[36] The people practically ignored the other gods. For example, on a stela in the falcon catacomb, Toth and Harendotes are represented along with Imhotep, but only Imhotep is addressed in the inscription.[37]

Nevertheless, Imhotep continued to be increasingly appealing to the intellectuals and people of high status during the Ptolemaic Period. Teos, the high priest of Memphis, addresses his prayers to Imhotep on his stela and acclaims him as he

... who calculates everything for the library; who restores what is found demolished in the holy books; who knows the secrets of the house of gold.[38]

Even later, during the reign of the Emperor Augustus, people of high status worshipped Imhotep. One of the best indications that they did so is provided by a group of tomb stelae dedicated by the members of the family of the high priest of Memphis (and now in the British Museum).[39] On the first stela[40] we see the high priest Psenptais worshipping the pantheon of the gods, and in the seventh position is

Imhotep, Son-of-Ptah, successful in his action, great in miracles.

Psenptais states

I was a great one, rich in everything, and I had a beautiful harim.

47

Fig. 32. Stela of Psenptais

Fig. 33. Stela of Taimhotep

I was forty-three years old without a male offspring. Then the majesty of this august god Imhotep, Son-of-Ptah gave me a male son without any fault and whose name was fixed to Imhotep named Petebastis. He was born by Taimhotep. . . .

On the second stela, Taimhotep speaks:

The heart of the high-priest rejoiced very much about our wedding. I was three times pregnant for him, but except for three daughters I did not bear him a male child. Then, together with the high priest, I implored the majesty of this august god, great in miracles, successful in his acts, who gives a son to whomever does not have one, to Imhotep, Son-of-Ptah. He heard our prayers. The majesty of this god stepped to the head of this high-priest with a revelation and spoke to him: Make a great work at the august place of $^c n^c$-t3.wj, the place, where my body is hidden. I shall recompense you for it with a son, a male one. Then he woke up and prostrated himself in front of this august god. . . .[41]

Psenptais erected a statue of Imhotep in north Saqqâra, and Taimhotep continues

As recompense he caused me to become pregnant with a boy; he was born. . . .

The son, named Petebastis, also alludes to this story on his own stela[42] and a namesake of about the same period mentions Imhotep's name on a statue base he dedicated to the god, now in the British Museum.[43] A calendar of feasts is carved on the base that describes in great detail the six stations in the life of Imhotep: his birth as son of Ptah and Khereduankh, his presentation in front of Ptah and Sachmet, the defeat of the Asiatics by Sachmet (the relevance of this event to Imhotep will be discussed further), his illness and death, mummification, and his apotheosis and proclamation as a god. The only good parallel to this calendar is a list of feasts of the deified King Amenhotep I of Ramesside times: birth, illness, death, and burial.[44] (A fragmentary demotic text of late Ptolemaic times, in Berlin, presents a late Memphite theology of Imhotep. It includes a calendar of feasts similar to the one we are discussing.)[45]

It was not until the time of the Roman Empire that Imhotep was

Fig. 34. Base of a statue of Imhotep and his mother

taken as a truly popular god of the masses. This is indicated by the fact that we find images devoted to him that are of a poor quality of workmanship. A stela from Mitrahina, in the Cairo Museum, shows Imhotep in front of a king, holding both the scepter and the sign of life.[46] Both now have been deified. The provenance and conception of the stela prove that it was used as an altar in a private house. There is a miniature chapel in the Cairo Museum[47] enclosing a sitting figure of Imhotep, and a similar figure in a private collection in Munich; the poor quality of the figures indicates the social levels of the owners. In addition, neither piece is inscribed, which may indicate that the pieces were mass produced, with no particular owner in mind, and probably sold in the sanctuary of Imhotep to anyone who wanted a figure for private use at home.

As we have seen, the cult of Imhotep was begun in Memphis, and by the time of the first of the Ptolemy's, his shrine had become a famous destination for pilgrims. His fame as an "effective god," at this time, also had spread all over Egypt, and, accordingly, a shrine was established in Heliopolis. (This cult was perhaps encouraged by the awareness that in much earlier times, Djoser, Imhotep's pharaoh, had constructed some buildings there.) Further to the north, a cult of Imhotep was established in Xois (Tell Sakha). Here his followers erected a stela in the first century A.D.,[48] which shows Imhotep in purely divine form, sitting in the same manner in which he was depicted on the altars of Mitrahina. The inscription calls him

> ... the holy child, born by Naunet, made by Nun ..., who makes safe the destroyed land, who makes great the small one, who satisfies the hungry, Imhotep-the-Great, Son-of-Ptah. May his name be praised in his town $^\text{H}$ **3 sww** eternally.

A fragment of a statue, now in the Musée Rodin in Paris,[49] is from Mendes, in the Delta, and was made in the early Ptolemaic Period for the priest Philotas of the early Ptolemaic Period. Philotas addresses Imhotep in the following words:

> I belong to your people, O Son-of-Ptah, born by Khereduankh, the daughter of the ram, the lord of Mendes.

He thanks Imhotep for having cured him. Incidentally, the connection between Imhotep and Mendes results from Imhotep's mother being born by the god of Mendes, the sacred ram. We can explain this

Fig. 35. Naos of Imhotep used as altar

in two ways: Either Khereduankh was really born *in* Mendes and was later given a divine father on the pattern of Ptah, father of Imhotep, or else she had no genuine connection with this place. She was put in relation to the ram on the analogy of Imhotep in his relation to Ptah so as to establish the cult of Imhotep theologically in Mendes.

In Alexandria, the Egyptians erected a statue of Imhotep, in an Hellenic style; he is depicted clad in a Greek costume.[50] He is holding a papyrus roll and accompanied by a baboon wearing the crescent and the moon disk. Another Hellenistic style figure shows the same baboon at the base of the scribes' statue, which we may assume is to be identified with Imhotep.[51] The cult of Imhotep spread to Athribis near the modern town of Benha, north of Cairo. He is referred to on a statue in the titles of a priest named Harpocrates found there.[52] A papyrus was uncovered in the Fayum (now in the Michaelides Collection),[53] which dates from the first or second century B.C. The name of Imhotep is mentioned several times in connection with the "Great One of Babylon" in the text, which is a romance. Another late demotic papyrus, now in Copenhagen, gives us a good parallel to the text in the Michaelides Collection showing how Imhotep has been made the hero of romances.[54] Imhotep is conducting a campaign with King Djoser against an Assyrian queen. In the story, he wins the battle by employing magical practices. To the popular mind, during the latest Egyptian times, Imhotep has become a sage and a magician, a historical person, and a divine being. He is the hero of pseudo-historical stories that had become popular at the time. (And we may remember the calendar of feasts of Imhotep on the statue base in London. There we met with a feast mentioning the defeat of the Asiatics by Sachmet. Perhaps there is some connection between this feast and the feasts of Imhotep in the story on this papyrus.)

Even at a later date than the papyri described above, the cult of Imhotep was followed in the south of Egypt, for he is presented in an unpublished scene in one of the Roman rock chapels at Tehna in Middle Egypt. He is sitting at the door of the small sanctuary being adored by a man in Hellenistic costume.[55] The importance of Imhotep at this place needs further investigation. His stature and role in late Egypt are made much more apparent in the great temple of Hathor in Dendera, where he is represented twice. In the first (unpublished) relief, Imhotep is found above the door opening through the west wall to the sacred lake.[56] He speaks to the Emperor Augustus:

54

I bring you Punt with all its treasures, I cause the Nile to come in time.

He is extolled as providing Egypt with the treasures of foreign countries and the fertility of the inundation; he guarantees the political and cosmic order. Second, Imhotep is praised in a long hymn on the left side of the jacade of the temple.[57] This dates from the time of the Roman Emperor Claudius who decorated a good part of the exterior walls of the Dendera temple:

> Veneration of Imhotep. Praise to you, O god, borne a god, divine offspring of Ptah, engendered in Memphis, august child, wonderful son of Khereduankh. . . . O Imhotep in your name "the wonderful," "the mighty," "of great reputation in the Two Lands," who restores what is destroyed everywhere in the temples, of perfect intelligence, who calculates everything, skillful like Toth, the great . . . successful in his activities, who knows the prescriptions and the recipes, which are written upon his heart, who lets be known the movement of the stars . . . who attenuates famine, skillful in his words, experienced in the divine writings, who gives life to the people and protects the pregnant, who gets the sterile with child, who gives a son to everyone who implores it, who protects the child, who regenerates the age of those who serve god, who soothes illness.
>
> Great, wonderful appearance which stays on earth; there are no troubles as long as he is to be seen every day. Your secret appearance is great in towns and nomes; your throne is high in the houses of the gods in the Two Lands. They rejoice if they see you hearing the prayers of everybody.
>
> Offerings for you, consisting of bread, meat, milk as a regular offering every day.

This part of a long text is by far the most detailed description of Imhotep's position in the theology and religion of Ptolemaic times.

The fact that the text is positioned on an outside wall near the main entrance of the temple is also significant. Imhotep is in this way signified to be the door god mediating between the religious people and the god of the temple. The inscription faces the so-called sanatorium of Dendera, the famous hospital for medical and magical cures, which was located at the right of the court of the temple. In this way, the Egyptians have conveyed the indirect relationship which was thought to obtain between Imhotep and the inscription. His inscription faces a block with a text which occurs elsewhere in the Temple of Debod, where it is recited by Imhotep himself in the temple of Debod.

Neither at Dendera nor at many of the other places at which Imhotep was worshipped did the Egyptians provide a proper sanctuary for his cult. The Egyptians provided him with a temple comparable to the one at Saqqâra only at Thebes (where he was given several). At first, the Egyptians acknowledged Imhotep only in the small temple of Ptah in the enclosure of Amun in Karnak. The temple was built by a Memphite cult settled at Karnak. In the time of Ptolemy III, Imhotep is represented in a small relief at the sixth gate of the temple.[58] He is placed between the king and Ptah, mediating at the door of the sanctuary. Nearby, the followers of Imhotep portray him in the small hypostyle hall of the same temple forming a triad with Ptah and Hathor.[59] But the inscription accompanying his figure continues to follow those found in Memphis:

Imhotep-the-Great, Son-of-Ptah, helpful god who comes to everybody imploring him, who gives everybody life.

On the exterior east wall of the temple of Ptah, a relief of Imhotep was carved of very good quality, showing in the middle Imhotep preceded by Hathor and little Harsomtus.[60] (The other figures were added later.) Around the relief we can see holes which once retained plugs of wood to support a light wooden building, a chapel added to the temple wall. In this chapel, the devotees of Imhotep could participate, very intimately, in the rituals and offerings of the main cult of Ptah. (One of the figures later added to this relief was that of Amenhotep, Son-of-Hapu, in dependency on Imhotep in spite of his Theban origin; his costume, his beard, his emblems, of a scribe's palette and a papyrus roll, prove his human character, whereas Imhotep is represented as a full divinity.) Still later, the Egyptians added another relief that included a figure of Ptah accompanied by a small figure of Imhotep. In this relief, the Egyptians have repartitioned the relief with Hathor in one part, Imhotep in the middle, and Amenhotep in the other; this arrangement corresponds with the sanctuaries behind this wall, the sanctuaries of Sakhmet, Ptah, and Amun. Imhotep is the representative of Ptah; Amenhotep is the intermediary for Amun.

56

Fig. 36. Temple of Ptah at Karnak, the first sanctuary of Imhotep at Thebes

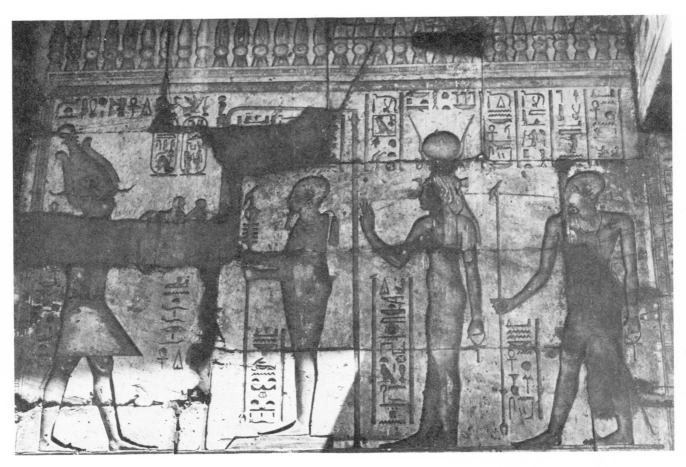

Fig. 37. Imhotep in the hypostyle of the temple of Ptah at Karnak

Under the reign of Tiberius a hymn to Imhotep was inscribed over the fourth gate of the temple of Ptah.[61] Some passages of this hieroglyphic text may give us an impression of its form and contents:

Praise to you, Imhotep . . . Come to your home, to your temple in Thebes. . . . May you get offerings here and smell incense, may your body be renewed by the libation.
This is your place; it is your favorite place. It is more useful for you than your place in other towns. . . . You can see the houses of the gods at all four sides of your house. You receive the offerings coming out from their offering-tables. The administrators of your divine domain bring you their offerings of every good

58

thing. . . . The men praise you, the wives do obeisance to you, and everybody without exception praises your success, for you are healing them. It is you who gives them life. . . . The sages praise god for you, and the first under them is your brother, your beloved, Amenhotep-the-Great, Son-of-Hapu. He is with you, and he is not far from you, so that your bodies are completely united and your *ka* receives the offerings which your son Kaisaros Sebastos brings you.

Then, quite near this center of worship of Imhotep, we find him once more north of the court dating from the Middle Kingdom. The

Fig. 38. East exterior wall of the temple of Ptah at Karnak

Fig. 39. Temple of Amun at Karnak, side room. Imhotep and his holy
community

Egyptians represented Imhotep here in a relief in the central part of the temple of Amon indicating that Imhotep was becoming even more widely revered.[62] Together with Amenhotep, he stands between Ptah and Ptolemy IX and is called

The helpful god, made by Tatenen, chief of the gold house.

Imhotep is portrayed accompanying Ptah and interceding for him just as they have entered the main temple of Amun.

By this time, the cult of Imhotep had also spread to the north of Karnak. A stela that once was fixed in a temple wall there in Roman times shows Imhotep and Amenhotep facing each other in the typical manner used on altars.[63] The relation of this stela to the temple of Imhotep's original cult, the temple of Ptah, is indicated by the inscription made to Imhotep:

Wonderful appearance of the gods.

We have already found this epithet to be typical of Memphis. Because the sanctuary of Imhotep, near the temple of Ptah, had become so important, it is reasonable to assume that a large figure of Imhotep said to have been found at Karnak belongs to this sanctuary.[64] It is a Roman-style figure (now in Amsterdam) and is identified by the inscription on the back pillar:

Son of Ptah, born by the beautiful singer Khereduankh, who cures the limbs of everybody.

(A priest of Imhotep named Psenmonthes, who is mentioned on a mummy label in Brooklyn that is said to come from Thebes, may also have belonged to this temple.[65])

The cult of Imhotep was not accepted, or did not gain any followers, on the west bank of Thebes before the time of Ptolemy IV. And when his cult was established, it occupied the second rank to his Theban colleague Amenhotep, who had been venerated on the west bank for more than a millennium. Imhotep was first *venerated* in the small temple of Dier el-Medineh on one of the columns of the hypostyle as the

. . . helpful god, born by Tatenen, wonderful appearance of the gods, who gives life to everybody attached to him.[66]

Fig. 40. Column in the ptolemaic temple of Deir el-Medineh.
Imhotep and his mother

He is accompanied for the first time by his family. Behind him in the costume of Hathor is his mother, "the god's mother and beautiful nurse Khereduankh," followed by his wife, the "god's sister Renpet-nefret" wearing the **rnp.t** sign on her head. Both are represented like goddesses, and the god referred to in their titles is Imhotep. (Khereduankh was probably an historical person; Renpet-nefret seems to have been a fictive person created to complete Imhotep's holy family.)

Some decades later the cult of Imhotep and Amenhotep spread to Deir el-Bahari. According to the building inscription there,[67] Ptolemy III had built a chapel to the Greek god Asclepius on the second terrace of the ruined temple of Queen Hetshepsut.[68] Many years later, Ptolemy VIII added a rock chapel behind the old temple and dug into the mountain.[69] At the entrance to these "new" subterranean rooms he built a light portico of six columns[70] The new sanctuary was decorated with reliefs and inscriptions which are clearly divided into two sections: to the left and on the south side those related to Imhotep; to the right and on the north side those for Amenhotep. Imhotep is standing on the south wall near the entrance to the room in front of an emblem of the nome of Thebes.[71] He is called

> ... the great chief lector-priest, the magnificent, Imhotep-the-Great, Son-of-Ptah ..., who hears the prayers in the west of Thebes, who completes the wealth of its inhabitants with flourishing life.

He is followed by his mother and his wife and then four lesser gods. Then, we can read in a final line:

> Imhotep, the august god, the greatest of the physicians, with skillful fingers for everybody imploring him.

And in the top line we read about him:

> The lector-priest, the servant of Toth, the physician ... who fixes the plans of the gods' temples.

We notice that the Egyptians in Thebes emphasize Imhotep's earthly titles, whereas in Karnak and, of course, in Memphis they worship his divinity. As time passed the Egyptians came to worship Amenhotep,

63

Fig. 41. Upper terrace of the temple of Hetshepsut at Deir el-Bahari. Ptolemaic colonnade in front of the sanctuary of Imhotep and Amenhotep

even more so than Imhotep, at the temple of Hetshepsut.[72] Imhotep is mentioned or referred to only infrequently in inscriptions and always under the name of his Greek counterpart Asclepius. We may even guess that the Ptolemies established a cult for Imhotep in western Thebes, but mostly to neutralize an important local deity. He was presented under the name of Asclepius because the sanctuary was visited mostly by Greeks. In addition, there is one location in western Thebes that gives us the impression that there was some popular veneration of Imhotep. It is on the exterior wall of the small temple of Medinet Habu, where we find some poor graffiti which show the figure or the head of Imhotep.[73] Surely they belong to Egyptian, not Greek, people, and they support the conclusion we made from Deir el-Bahari that they were ancient Egyptian cults.

Eventually, the worship of Imhotep spread to the provinces, far from the Hellenistic center of Thebes.[74] In the bull catacombs in the Bucheum at Armant, which was a popular cult site the Egyptians show Imhotep sitting in his classical attitude on a small stela. The inscription consists of a hymn:

64

Fig. 42. Ptolemaic room in the temple of Hetshepsut. Imhotep is on the left wall

Praise to you, Imhotep-the-Great, Son-of-Ptah, borne by Kereduankh, made by Tatenen. He gives good . . . to give life. . . .

The fact that the Egyptians constructed a small cult place for Imhotep the healer in the bull catacombs of the Bucheum was perhaps influenced by the cult of Imhotep near the bull catacombs of Serapeum in Saqqâra.

The cult spread south of Thebes as well. Imhotep is mentioned in a text that originated in Esna in the time of Domitian.[75] Imhotep is said to "cure any illness according to its nature." However, of even greater importance, the Egyptians memorialized Imhotep from the time of Ptolemy VI to Ptolemy XI, several times in the temple of Horus at Edfu.[76] In the vestibule to the treasury beside the door leading to the sacred well, we see Ptolemy VI making offering "for his august father" and "for the chief lector-priest."[77] No name is given, but the god is represented in the right half of the wall; this is Imhotep in his normal divine appearance, called

. . . great god, residing at Edfu, at whose order everybody lives, who cures any illness in Egypt.

In accompanying texts, Imhotep promises the king regular inundations of the Nile and the products of Punt and Byblos. These inscriptions and the representation of Imhotep are very similar to those at Dendera, and the Egyptians placed them in exactly the same location in both temples, at the doorway leading to the sacred lake. The Egyptians carved a representation of Imhotep on the so-called Library of the Temple of Horus (a small room in the pronaos where the holy books were stored).[78] He wears a panther skin and stands in front of Horus with his arms lowered in devout adoration. Here the Egyptians have combined all of the qualities attributed to Imhotep. In the carving they show Imhotep no longer as a god addressed by another, but speaking to the god of the temple. They show him in a historical role as the chief lector-priest, and this is the title given him on this relief. In addition, they call him by his normal epithet, Son-of-Ptah. Then, Ptolemy IX describes the building activities of Imhotep in the inscriptions that were carved around the inner side of the enclosure wall:

He [the king] protected the temple by this wall on four sides,

Fig. 43. Building inscription in the temple of Edfu

according to the book of the order of the temple which was made by the chief lector-priest Imhotep-the-Great, Son-of-Ptah.[79]

In this inscription, from Ptolemaic times, the Egyptians continued to attribute to Imhotep the principles of temple architecture, exactly as they had on the statue base from Saqqâra I discussed earlier. The determinative of "chief lector-priest" indicates that the Egyptians still thought of Imhotep as the chief ritualist as well. The feathers on his head, not otherwise used in Egyptian reliefs, are mentioned by the Christian author, Clement of Alexandria in his description of an Egyptian temple feast:

Fig. 44. Imhotep's determinative in the building
inscription

The holy scribe . . . , who has feathers on his head, in his hand a book and a box which contains black ink and a reed to write with it.[80]

The Egyptians conveyed the mythical aspects of Imhotep in an inscription at the end of the text on the temple wall. The book with the order of the temple is described as having fallen directly from heaven, north of Memphis.[81] The historical origin of the book is transposed into a mythical one, and the location preserves some relation to Imhotep. On the west enclosure wall, the Egyptians carved the different acts of the myth of Horus.[82] In the final scene, Seth in the

Fig. 45. Imhotep as chief lector in the Horus myth. Edfu, enclosure wall

shape of a hippopotamus is slaughtered by a butcher, and the chief lector-priest recites the magic formulae. And he is described as

> the chief lector-priest, the scribe of the book of god, Imhotep-the-Great, Son-of-Ptah.[83]

Imhotep is wearing a long coat and a panther's skin and holds the papyrus roll. In this essential, final phase of the myth, no ordinary, anonymous chief lector-priest may act, only the most famous, well known for thousands of years: Imhotep.

Further south from Edfu on the island of Sehel in the middle of the first cataract south of Aswan is carved a famous text that mentions Imhotep. The inscription is thirty-two lines long and is dated to the eighteenth year of king Djoser of the Third Dynasty, although it is clearly Ptolemaic in style and language.[84] The text reports a famine of seven years duration which occurred in the reign of Djoser. The king asks Imhotep what to do. Imhotep then consults the "House of Life" in Hermopolis, after which he explains that the Nile comes from Elephantine and gives a detailed description of the topographical and mineralogical features of the region of Aswan. He then states that Khnum is the god responsible for the inundation, whereupon Khnum appears before the king and sends water. Djoser dedicates all of the land twelve miles south of Elephantine to the god and awards him all of the transit taxes from this area.[85] But here the Egyptians have shown Imhotep as the wise man who knows everything, or at least who knows in which library to look for the answer! He also has special knowledge which enables him to enumerate about thirty different types of stones and minerals that are extracted in the cataract region—typical of an architect who used Aswan granite as a building material for the first time.

On the island of Philae, near Sehel, Ptolemy V erected a small temple for Imhotep consisting of two undecorated rooms.[86] The facade bears two registers of very fine reliefs, and above the doorway there is a short dedication in Greek:

> The king Ptolemy and queen Cleopatra, the gods made manifest, and Ptolemy, their son, for Asclepius.[87]

They dedicated the temple when their son, Ptolemy VI, was born after seven years of childless marriage. Imhotep, who is called Asclepius only in the dedication, has acted in his well-known capacity.

70

Fig. 46. Famine stela on Sehel island

Fig. 47. The temple of Imhotep at Philae

But here we also find an interesting analogy to the monument at Sehel. At Sehel, Imhotep ended seven years of drought; here he ends seven years of childlessness. The front of the temple of Imhotep at Philae also portrays him leaving his house and receiving the offerings presented by the king. Most of the inscriptions related to Imhotep are identical with those known from other places; he is accompanied by his mother, Khereduankh, who is called "beloved by the ram, the lord of Mendes," as she was at Mendes. But, at Philae, Imhotep is uniquely called "august appearance of Khnum, master of Elephantine." Sometimes striding, sometimes sitting, Imhotep here combines in his iconography all the different forms of his cult in Egypt.

Imhotep's shrine at Philae was dedicated by a king, but it still did not receive much attention—at any rate, worshippers have left few inscriptions or graffiti.[88] The Egyptians, however, did include him in the official theology of Philae, and he was mentioned at several locations in the main temple of Isis: on the first pylon, on the gate of Ptolemy II (decorated under Tiberius), the mamisi, and in the hypostyle hall.[89] In the inscriptions we find here, Imhotep is extolled for his powers to provide health and fertility:

> Master of life, who gives it to everyone who loves him, by whom everyone lives; master of health, who cures the limbs, who revivifies people in the state of death, who brings up the egg in the belly.

The Egyptians acknowledge his influence over the fertility of nature:

> . . . who gives everything which comes out of Geb and sprouts on the back of the earth, who gives everything which he has produced by his own hands.

The Egyptians also claim Imhotep to be an expert in astronomy, as they did in the inscription at Dendera. Much later, these inscriptions will, in part, form the basis on which the Egyptians came to accept Imhotep as a famous astrologer.

The popularity that the cult of Imhotep was beginning to enjoy at Philae influenced the Nubians, further south, to adopt the cult. Thus, soon after Ptolemy V built his small temple, the Meroitic king Adikhalamani, the predecessor of Ergamenes, constructed a chapel at Debod.[90] At the doorway to this temple, Imhotep is shown following the god Toth on the one side and Horus on the other:

The chief royal scribe, the sage, great in the whole land.

In the inscription, he addresses the king, as he enters the room, with a long speech in which he transfigures the limbs of the king's body into holy entities. He is also described as acting as the chief ritualist, the magician. Imhotep also was presented in the Roman forecourt of the temple.[91] (The figure is now almost completely destroyed, but it can be seen in publications of the early nineteenth century.[92]) The texts are completely in the tradition of Philae.

Somewhat later, and further south from Debod, the Egyptians included Imhotep in the Ptolemaic temple of Kalabsha. On the blocks of this temple, now in Berlin, he is referred to as

Imhotep-the-Great, Son-of-Ptah, the chief lector-priest, helpful god, born by Tatenen.[93]

He stands before a king (whose name was usurped by a king called Romaios Kaisaros Theos, that is, Augustus). Behind Imhotep stands Kereduankh whose words are exactly the same as those inscribed in the hypostyle of Philae. Imhotep is also represented on the south wall of one of the vestibules.[94] He is represented symmetrically with the

Fig. 48. Court of the temple of Debod. Ancient drawing of a destroyed scene

figure of the god Tutu, a popular divine messenger at the time who appears in the company of Imhotep in some reliefs at Philae. This representation of Imhotep is the only one in which his skin is painted blue; this was done perhaps, to indicate his cosmic qualities or his function as the bringer of the Nile.

Apparently the southernmost temple was constructed to Imhotep at Dakka, about 150 kilometers south of Philae. There the Meroitic king Ergamenes built a chapel soon after Adikhalamani had built a temple to Imhotep at Debod, and followed much the same plan. Imhotep is located on the same walls, as he was at Debod. Here, however, he is one of the gods of the temple, not the acting ritualist.[95] The inscriptions are almost the same in both temples.

Imhotep had no separate following of his own in Nubia. The cult of Imhotep was never very strong, and limited to the official theology, not the practiced religion. There was no community of worshippers as there was in Memphis. Nevertheless, any theology which wanted to claim to be complete had to acknowledge him, and we therefore can find him represented in almost all of the important temples of Ptolemaic times. (Where we cannot find him, as at Kom Ombo, for example, we may assume that this is due to the state of the preservation of the temple.) It is not astonishing, therefore, to encounter Imhotep at Meroe, in the decorated chamber of pyramid N. 12,[96] and to see him in an early Ibis tomb in the Oasis of Bahriya.[97] Here he acts as the earthly representative of the god Thoth, but is quite normally

Imhotep-the-Great, Son-of-Ptah.

Thus, Imhotep appears in the temples of Upper Egypt and Nubia almost exclusively in temple reliefs in the official theology. There are only a few indications that he was worshipped by the people—in the Bucheum, for example, or, of course, at Thebes. This is the essential difference between his cult at Memphis and those everywhere else.

The late Greek and early Roman historians, who flourished at the end of the genuine Egyptian era continued to link the name of Imhotep closely with Memphis. But Diodorus confused Imhotep with the Greek hero and inventor of architecture, Daedalus. He does ascribe to him the building of the temple at Memphis and calls him the son of Hephaestus (which means Ptah). And Diodorus was also correctly aware of the privilege Imhotep had been awarded of erecting a statue of his own in the temple (we recall the statue base at Saqqâra) and of the veneration in which he was held because of his good

Fig. 49. Sanctuary of the temple of Dakka

character. Finally Diodorus mentions Imhotep's tomb on a hill near Memphis, greatly esteemed by the local people.

The most important Greek text concerning Imhotep is contained on a papyrus from Oxyrhynchos, written around the second century A.D.[98] It contains a theological treatise on Imhotep within a pseudo-historical romance.

The story is set in the time of Nectanebos, when an Egyptian papyrus was found in the abandoned Memphite temple of Asclepius. The king asked a priest to translate the text into Greek because he had heard that this god was already greatly venerated by King Mycerinus. But the translation proved to be so difficult that the priest gave up, and this provoked the revenge of the god himself. The priest, accordingly, fell ill, and, after some time, the god appeared to him and his mother in a vision. He was of superhuman size, in a bright white garment, holding a book in his left hand. The priest thereupon resumed his work and praised the god in the following words:

As the inventor of writing, O Asclepius, greatest of the gods, as the teacher of writings you are greatly esteemed by the gratitude of all people. Any votive-stela, any offering-gift lasts only for a moment and perishes immediately; but a book is an immortal recompense which over time is renewed in the memory.
Every Greek tongue will report your story, and every Greek man will venerate the son of Ptah, Imuthes.

This is almost a Greek version of the *Harper's Song!* The Greeks made a clear identification of Imhotep with Asclepius, but they gave him a special name in Greek, Imuthes. They also point out that the fame of Imhotep spread amongst the Greek population:

Every Greek tongue will report your story, and every Greek man will venerate the son of Ptah, Imuthes.[99]

In several other late Greek and Latin texts, Imhotep is described as a former human being who had become esteemed as a god in Memphis.[100] But the late Hermitic literature begins to pay some attention to Imhotep as a healer, sage, and magician (as had the Egyptians), and he becomes more important eventually in the latter role.[101] There is a papyrus in the British Museum that gives detailed instructions on how to use Imhotep in magical practices.[102] The Christian writer Jerome describes a school of magic sciences at Memphis, which was directed by the prophets of Imhotep.[103] The magical iconography survived on into the fifth century A.D., which marked the end of the ancient traditions about Imhotep. But this was not his end in the memory of men.

After nearly five centuries we again find Imhotep written about, this time in Arabic texts of the tenth century.[104] The alchemist Ibn Umayl, who lived in the first half of the tenth century, reports a trip he made to a place called Busir, where he visited a building known as the "prison of Joseph."[105] In part, he describes

. . . a stone figure which is sitting in the temple beside the doorway to the left of the entrance facing the entering people, sitting on a seat like that used by the physician, manufactured separately from the statue. And on his lap, on both his forearms, both hands over his knees, was a tablet, also made separately. Its length was one cubit, its breadth one span, and the fingers of the hands of the statue below the tablet were holding the tablet.

76

SENIOR PHILOSOPHVS.

Quid Soles, Lunæ signent, pictæue tabellæ,
 Quid uenerandi etiam, proflua barba, Senis.
Turba quid astantum, uolucrum quid turba uolantū,
 Antra quid, armati quid pedes usq; uolent.
Miraris? Veterum sunt hæc monumenta Sophorum,
 Omnia consignans, iste Libellus habet.

Fig. 50. Imhotep as Alchemist. Renaissance drawing

And the tablet was like a book, open to everybody entering as if it should signal to the people: Look at it! And on the side of the statue, I mean in the hall of the temple, were many pictures of many different things and inscriptions.
And the tablets on the lap of the stone sculpture was divided in the middle in two halves. . . .

Ibn Umayl then gives a long, very detailed description of the inscriptions and pictures on the tablet, which he then explains as magical signs. (In one of the oldest printed editions of this text, dating from the sixteenth century, we even find a representation of the figure of Imhotep; later editions copy the figure but alter it to such an extent that it can hardly be recognized.) No doubt we have here a description of Imhotep with his inscribed papyrus roll. The figure was still standing in the tenth century A.D. when it was studied by Arab scholars as an essential source of alchemical science. Even the word used by Ibn Umayl to describe the building, barba^c, is of pharaonic origin. It was derived from the coptic *PERPE,* which, in turn, comes from the Egyptian **p3-r3-pr,** "the temple."

Busir, mentioned by Ibn Umayl, is also mentioned by several other Arab writers as the location of the sanctuary for Imhotep.[106] From these different texts we can deduce that Busir was the name for the modern village of Abusir, and the exact position of the temple is described as being on a hill nearby. We cannot describe the reason why the temple was referred to as the prison of the Biblical Joseph, but we should point out that this prison of Joseph, the ancient temple of Imhotep, was still greatly venerated by the people of Saqqâra into the middle of the nineteenth century and continued to be visited by pilgrims who left their graffiti on the walls of a small Muslim chapel nearby.[107]

NOTES

1. K. Sethe, "Heroes and Hero-Gods," in *Hastings Encyclopedia of Religion and Ethics* (1913), 646-652.
2. For the bibliography of these and

other "saints," see D. Wildung, *o.c.,* 74, n.1.
3. For the general historical background, *CAH* I/2,[3] (1971), 1–70, 145–160.
4. The basic study about Imhotep is

still K. Sethe, *Imhotep—Der Asklepios der Ägypter,* (UGAÄ II/4), Leipzig, 1902; for a good popular account, see J. B. Hurry, *Imhotep—The Vizier and Physician of King Zoser and Afterwards the Egyptian God of Medicine,* Oxford,[2] 1928, with bibliography on pp. 185–189.

5. JE 49889: C. M. Firth, *ASAE* 26 (1926), 99–100, pl. 1; B. Gunn, *ASAE* 26 (1926), 177–196; J.-Ph. Lauer, *Histoire monumentale des pyramides* I (1962), 171–176, pl. 35.

6. P. Kaplony, *Inschriften der ägyptischen Frühzeit* I (1963), 403–404.

7. *PM* V, 196; R. Engelbach, *JEA* 20 (1934), 183–184, pl. 24.

8. H. Schäfer, *Ein Bruchstück altägyptischer Annalen* (1902), 26.

9. Z. Goneim, *Horus Sekhem-Khet* (1957), 4, pl. 13.

10. K. Sethe, *Imhotep,* 7.

11. For a concise account of Emery's excavations and the recent work, see H. S. Smith, *A Visit to Ancient Egypt* (1974).

12. *PM* V, 72; J. H. Breasted, *Ancient Records* I (1906), 143, § 312, with n.d.

13. A. Erman, *Die Märchen des Papyrus Westcar* (1890); W. K. Simpson (ed.), *The Literature of Ancient Egypt*[2] (1973), 15 ff.

14. W. K. Simpson (ed.), *o.c.,* 16, with n.1.

15. *PM* I[2], 456 (4).

16. A. H. Gardiner, *ZÄS* 40 (1902), 146.

17. M. Lichtheim, *JNES* 4 (1945), 178–212; W. K. Simpson (ed.), *o.c.,* 306.

18. *Ibid.,* 340. E.g. J. H. Breasted, *The Edwin Smith Surgical Papyrus* I (1930), 9, 75.

19. A. H. Gardiner, *Hieratic Papyri in the British Museum,* 3rd Series (1935), I, 38–40; II, pl. 19; A.

Erman (ed. W. K. Simpson), *The Ancient Egyptians* (1966, XVII; W. K. Simpson (ed.), *o.c.,* 1.

20. J. Yoyotte, *BSFE* 11 (1952), 67–72; W. K. Simpson (ed.), *o,c.,* fig. 6 (only one half).

21. A. H. Gardiner, *The Royal Canon of Turin* (1959), 15–16, n. III 6 , 17, pl. 9, no. 40.

22. *Ibid.,* pl. 2, no. 18a.

23. W. G. Waddell (ed.), *Manetho* (1964), 40–45.

24. Berlin 14765; D. Wildung, *Die Rolle ägyptischer Könige im Bewusstsein ihrer Nachwelt* (1969), 79–83, pl. 6–8.

25. *PM* VI, 335; D. Wildung, *o.c.,* 83–84.

26. Louvre N. 4541; unpublished, mentioned here with kind permission by the late J. Vandier. See Ch. Boreux, *Guide-catalogue* (1932), 462.

27. Boston MFA 35.1484; *PM* II[2], 262; *E. Brummer Collection* (Sotheby Catalogue), November 16th, 17th, 1964, 38, no. 93.

28. Château Borély 46 (246): *Le Nil et la Société Égyptienne* (Exhibition December 1972—March 1973) (1972), no. 173.

29. Vatican 163–164: G. Botti—P. Romanelli, *Le sculture del Museo Gregoriano Egizio* (1951), 41–43, no. 42, pl. 34–36.

30. Brooklyn Museum L 68.10.1: R. Mond—O. Myers, *Temples of Armant* (1940), 51, 190, pl. 18,6.

31. P. Tresson, *Kêmi* 4 (1931), 144–150, pl. 7a.

32. E. Kiessling, *AfP* 15 (1953), 32–33; U. Wilcken, *Urkunden der Ptolemäerzeit* I, 40ff., 523ff., 589ff.

33. H. S. Smith, *A Visit to Ancient Egypt* (1974), 21–63.

34. As for example on one in the Brit. Mus. 1032 (375): *PM* III, 214;

Paris, Louvre C 119: P. Pierret, *Recueil d' inscriptions* II (1878), 12.

35. *JEA* 51 (1965), pl. 5.

36. *Dem Pap.* Louvre 2423: U. Wilcken, *UPZ*, 621.

37. W. B. Emery, *JEA* 57 (1971), 5–6, pl. 5, 4.

38. Vienna 154: *PM* III, 214.

39. *PM* III, 201; J. Quaegebeur, *Ancient Society* 3 (1972), 82–98.

40. Brit. Mus. 1026 (886).

41. Brit. Mus. 1027 (147); E. Otto, *Biographische Inschriften* (1954), 190–194, no. 57.

42. Brit. Mus. 1030 (188).

43. Brit. Mus. 512: H. Gauthier, *BIFAO* 14 (1918), 33–49, pl. 1.

44. W. Helck, in *Festschrift Schott* (1968), 71–72.

45. *Pap. Dem.* Berlin 13603: W. Erichsen—S. Schott, *Fragmente memphitischer Theologie in demotischer Schrift* (1954).

46. Cairo JE 34205. G. Maspero, *Le Musée Egyptien* I (1900), 44, pl. 46.

47. Cairo JE 31182. Unpublished.

48. Cairo JE 45701: *PM* IV, 45.

49. H. De Meulenaere, *CdE* 41/81 (1966), 42–46, 48–49, fig. 2–4.

50. Now in Turin, Museo di Antichità 269: A. Adriani, *Repertorio d' Arte dell' Egitto Greco-Romano*, Serie A II (1961), 61–62, no. 209, pl. 98.

51. Turin, *Museo de Antichità*, 688: *ibid.*; 63, no. 210, pl. 98.

52. A. Rowe, *New Light on Aegypto-Cyrenaean Relations,* (Suppl. ASAE 12), (1948), 69–76, pl. 14.

53. I am indebted to Mrs. U. Kaplony-Heckel for full information about this text.

54. D. Wildung, *Die Rolle ägyptischer Könige im Bewusstsein ihrer Nachwelt* (1969), 91–93.

55. Speos C: *PM* IV, 129, C (2)–(3).

56. Position *PM* V-I, 44 (240). Prof. F. Daumas provided me an excellent copy of this and the following text.

57. Position *PM* VI, 44 between (1) and (2). *TT* 355: *PM* I², 429.

58. *PM* II², 199 (12) (c)I, (d)I; *Urk.* VIII, 146–147, no. 217.

59. *PM* II², 199 (14); *LD* IV, 15d; *Urk.* VIII, 150, no. 231.

60. *PM* II², 201 (35).

61. *PM* II², 197 (4) (d); S. Sauneron, *BIFAO* 63 (1965), 73–87.

62. *PM* II², 104 (312) 3.

63. *PM* II², 15 (60). Unpublished. S. Sauneron gave me his kind permission to publish this relief.

64. Allard Pierson Museum 7876: *PM* II², 280.

65. N. Reich, *Studies Griffith* (1932), 167–170, pl. 70c (facing p. 442).

66. *PM* II², 402 (8).

67. *PM* II², 367 (145) (g)–(h).

68. *PM* II², 343.

69. *PM* II², 367–368 (145)–(148); E. Naville, *The Temple of Deir el-Bahri* V (1906), 11–12, pl. 148–150.

70. *PM* II², 365 (127).

71. *PM* II², 367 (146).

72. A. Bataille, *Les inscriptions grecques du temple de Hatshepsout à Deir el-Bahari* (1951).

73. Not completely published. Cf. W. F. Edgerton, *Medinet Habu Graffiti Facsimiles* (1937), pl. 5, no. 19–20; no. 66.

74. Brit. Mus. 59449. *PM* V, 159.

75. S. Sauneron, *Esna* II (1963), 211, no. 107.

76. For Imhotep's role in Edfu see E. Chassinat, *BIFAO* 28 (1929), 1ff.

77. *PM* VI, 140 (141a); *Edfou* II, 270, pl. 42a.

78. *PM* VI, 134 (96d); *Edfou* III, 341, pl. 59.

79. *PM* VI, 165 (324)–(326); *Edfou* VI, 10.

80. *Stromateis* VI, 4; cf. M. Berthelot, *Les origines de l'alchimie* (1885), 40–44.

81. *Edfou* VI, 6, 4.

82. *PM* VI, 161 (309)–(311).

83. *Edfou* VI, 87–90; X, pl. 146; XIII, pl. 514. M. Alliot, *Le culte d'Horus á Edfou* II (1954), 779–803.

84. The so-called Famine-Stela: *PM* V, 252, no. 81; P. Barguet, *La stèle de la famine à Séhel* (1953); D. Wildung, *Die Rolle ägyptischer Könige im Bewusstsein ihrer Nachwelt* (1969), 85–91.

85. K. Sethe, *Dodekaschoinos* (1901), 19–26.

86. *PM* VI, 211–212.

87. *LD* IV, 18; A. Bernand, *Les inscriptions grecques de Philae* I (1969), 99–109, pl. 32.

88. F. L. Griffith, *Catalogue of the Demotic Graffiti of the Dodecaschoenus* I (1937), 110, no. 405–406; II, 1935, pl. 62, no. 405–406.

89. *PM* VI, 217 (102); H. Junker, *Philä* I, 257–259, fig. 149–150. *PM* VI, 213–214 (65); *LD* IV, 75a. *PM* VI, 222 (194), 229 (236); E. Winter, *Philä* II (1965), 68–69, 252–253. *PM* VI, 234 (279); unpublished.

90. *PM* VII, 4 (17)–(18).

91. *PM* VII, 3 (9)–(10).

92. J. J. Rifaud, *Voyage en Egypte* (1829), pl. 175 (upper).

93. Unpublished. I am indebted to D. Arnold for photographs of these blocks.

94. *PM* VII, 16 (44).

95. *PM* VII, 47 (41), (45).

96. *PM* VII, 249; S. Chapman—D. Dunham, *Decorated Chapels of the Meroitic Pyramids* (1952), pl. 10 C.

97. *PM* VII, 307; A. Fakhry, *Bahria Oasis* II (1950), 30, fig. 15.

98. Pap. Oxyrhynchos 1381. B. Grenfell—A. Hunt (ed.), *The Oxyrhynchus Papyri* XI (1915), 221–234.

99. F. W. Speyer, *JbAC* 11/12 (1968/69), 26–41.

100. E.g. Tacitus, *Hist.* IV, 84; Clement, *Strom.*, I, 21, 314.1; Zosimos; Ammianus Marcellinus, *Res Gestae* XXII, 14.7; Cyril, *Contra Julianum* VI, 812; Proclus, *Commentary on Timaeus,* 49 A.

101. *Asclepius* III, 37; *Hermetica* XXIII, 6 (=Stobaios I, 49. 44); XXVI, 9 (=Stob. I, 49. 69).

102. K. Preisendanz, *Papyri Graecae Magicae* II (1931), 29.

103. *Vita Hilarionis,* 21. *Calvitii Encomium,* 10.

104. For the Arab traditions, see the comprehensive study of B. H. Stricker, "La prison de Joseph," *Acta Orientalia* 19 (1942), 100–137.

105. Stricker, *o.c.,* 101–118; cf. J. Ruska, *Isis* 24/67 (1935–36), 311–319.

106. Stricker, *o.c.*

107. A. Rhoné, *L'Egypte à petites journées* (1877), 257–258.

CHAPTER THREE

Amenhotep, Son-of-Hapu

Amenhotep, Son-of-Hapu appears as a colleague of Imhotep in almost all of the documents related to Imhotep that originated from Thebes.[1] The hymn to Imhotep inscribed in the temple of Ptah at Karnak indicates the relationship:

> Your brother, your beloved whom you love, Amenhotep-the-Great, Son-of-Hapu, he is with you, he is not far from you, so that your bodies are united completely. . . .

The interrelationship of Imhotep and Amenhotep developed only after the cult of Imhotep was established at Thebes. Before this, of course, Amenhotep evolved from a mortal to a god separately, during the last centuries of Egyptian history. We know more about the life of Amenhotep than we do of Imhotep, and therefore we can trace the development by means of which the Egyptians elevated a mortal from the historical individual to the mythical and finally to the divine in more detail than we can that of Imhotep.[2]

Amenhotep was born about 1450 B.C. in the time of Tuthmosis III at Athribis near the modern town of Benha, about forty kilometers north of Cairo. His father was a nobleman named Hapu, his mother the lady Itu. Amenhotep spent fifty years of his life in his native town where he held the titles of "king's scribe and chief of the priests of

Horus-Khentikheti," the local god of Athribis. From this period of his life, we have found an unpublished statue of Amenhotep at Athribis, and it shows him in the attitude of a scribe.[3]

The reigning king, Amenhotep III, called Amenhotep to the royal court at Thebes, when he was in his early fifties.[4] Amenhotep immediately became active as an architect and achieved the rank of the king's chief architect. From his inscriptions we can deduce that he also was a scribe and achieved the rank of "real first scribe of the king," a rank which we can describe as "minister of culture" for education, science, and cult, as well as being responsible for mining and building. Amenhotep also served as the steward to the king's daughter Sat-Amun and the organizer of the king's jubilees—duties normally performed by the eldest son of the king. His rise was rapid, and Amenhotep's inscriptions indicate that the appointments were extraordinary.

We know about ten statues from the surroundings of Karnak on which the activities of Amenhotep are described.[5] Four of them were found in different temples around Karnak[6] and two directly beside the main entrance on the south of the temple of Amun at the doorway of the tenth pylon.[7]

Amenhotep describes his various roles and duties in the inscriptions carved on his statues:

A really excellent scribe, the first in calculating everything, who gives for millions of people and counts for thousands, whose reed summarizes hundreds of thousands.

Eloquent and of satisfying sayings. One who was promoted by the quality of his plans. One whom the king has exalted over his equals, whose excellent character is known in the Two Lands. The really beloved of the king, who enters the heart of the king, whose intelligence promoted his family; the king's scribe Amenhotep. . . .

Amenhotep says of himself:

I am really magnificent among any people, one with a hearing heart when he is looking for a plan in some unknown problem, like one whose heart knows it already; who finds a sentence even if it was found destroyed; master of wisdom, friend of the ruler, who does useful things for the Horus, who makes his monu-

84

Fig. 51. Amenhotep as a scribe

Fig. 52. Amenhotep at the age of 80

ments splendid in order to cause everybody to remember him for ever at the august place.

Who guides the ignorant through the events since the primeval times, who shows their place to everybody who forgot about it; useful in his ideas, when he is looking for monuments to make immortal the name of his lord; who relates the proverb and acts with his fingers; leader of mankind, of engaging manners as a pleasant one. Who venerates the name of the king and his power, who praises his Majesty at any time of the day, who is on his guard in all his decisions. . . .

Amenhotep addresses himself:

> You go out to the sky and you cross the brazen one; you are united with the stars, and one acclaims you in the boat of the sun-god.

Amenhotep achieved his position in this world through his personal intellectual and moral qualities. But he also understood how to apply his abilities to assure a high position in his afterlife. First he sought permission from the king to place his statues in the temple of Amun. By this means, he transposed his earthly function of mediator between the crowd of simple people and the king to the religious and saintly function of an intermediary between the people and Amun. Thus, the inscription on his statue at the tenth pylon exhorts the people:

> O people of Karnak who wish to see Amun, come to me! I will transmit your requests, because I am the herald of this god. Nab-maat-Re [Amenhotep III] has given me the order to report to him everything which is told in this land.

Amenhotep also offers to act as an intermediary through his inscription on his statue near the tenth pylon:

> You people from Upper and lower Egypt, with your eyes watching the sun, you who are all coming to Thebes downstream and upstream in order to implore the lord of the gods, come to me! I transmit your words to Amun in Karnak. Give me an offering and pour a libation for me, because I am an intermediary nominated by the king to hear the requests of the suppliant, to report to him the desires of Egypt.

The fact that the people did rely upon Amenhotep to act as an intermediary for them with Amun is indicated by the fact that the inscriptions on the papyrus roll Amenhotep holds are almost completely worn down. The worshippers touched the inscriptions in order to come into closer contact with the saint. Needless to say, it requires a great many touches to obliterate heiroglyphs deeply incised in granite.

Amenhotep did continue to fulfill his earthly functions until he was well into his seventies. He was recorded to have built the temple of Soleb for the king's first jubilee. It was built far to the south, between the second and third cataract in upper Nubia. Here he is represented in the temple relief participating in the festival itself.[8] Amenhotep probably built the temples for the king's second and third jubilees as well.

In the thirty-fourth year of Amenhotep III Amenhotep died. He had spent more than thirty years at the royal court; he was about eighty years of age.

At the beginning of his career at Thebes, when he was still of humble circumstances and unsure of what would happen to him, Amenhotep prepared a tomb in the hill of Qurnat Murr^{c}ai in western Thebes.[9] Different types of funerary cones are known from this tomb on which he mentions his native town, his father, and some of his titles; he also uses his nickname Hui.[10] After he had begun to meet with success, Amenhotep abandoned this tomb and started to build a new tomb that would be more appropriate in shape and locale to his new position. We can assume that this tomb can be identified with the so-called "hanging tomb," high up on the cliffs behind Deir el-Medineh in a small, dark corner of the mountain called the Vallée de l'Aigle.[11] It was near the Valley of the Kings. In addition, the plan of this tomb corresponds to those of the royal tombs of the eighteenth Dynasty and later. For these reasons we can make the assumption that this was, indeed, Amenhotep's final tomb. (The poor state of the preservation of the two granite sarcophagi can be explained by the fact that tomb robbers threw them down the cliff from the tomb, which was located about twenty-five meters up in the overhanging rock.[12]

Amenhotep was given permission to build his tomb on the royal plan near the royal tombs, a privilege accorded only to a few princes and queens.[13] He even was permitted to build a temple that was larger than some of the royal mortuary temples in western Thebes. This indicates that Amenhotep had left behind him the domain of the simple mortals even before he had died. In the few preserved reliefs

Fig. 53. Temple of Soleb, built by Amenhotep

from this temple, Amenhotep is portrayed as an old man in a large, rounded wig. Age has been made an iconographic feature to express his wisdom. The wig was made a characteristic to identify him. The Egyptians originated this pictorial type in two statues near the tenth pylon, which they venerated as early as the Ramesside Period.

Then Amenhotep is portrayed, in his wig, in the tomb of Ramose.[14] He sits among the guests at a dinner given by Ramose in honor of his colleagues from the highest administration and along side of his namesake Amenhotep, high steward of Memphis. It is difficult to decide if Amenhotep, Son-of-Hapu is assisting at the dinner, as a living person, or if he is an important person from the immediate past who participates in the dinner magically.

A figure, called Hui and wearing a wig, can be seen in the Ramesside tomb 359 of In-her-khaui.[15] The figure holds the scribes' palette and reed and squats in the scribes' position behind a long row of ancient kings who are venerated by the owner of the tomb. This association indicates that the scribe is also held to be a local saint in Thebes. Of course, the name Hui, the titles, and the iconographic type all attest that this is Amenhotep. We have here the first clear evidence that Amenhotep, Son-of-Hapu was venerated posthumously as a local saint in western Thebes. (The importance of the veneration

Fig. 54. Amenhotep in the tomb of Ramose at Thebes

of Amenhotep is underlined by the fact that the Egyptians made a duplicate of the scene on an ostracon now in Berlin.[16])

The cult of Amenhotep, Son-of-Hapu was attended by clergy in his Theban mortuary temple late into the New Kingdom, and several of the priests are mentioned in connection with tomb robberies.[17] Apparently, these priests were from a low level of society and sometimes quite simple craftsmen serving in the temple guilds. However, the cult of Imhotep persisted and maintained some vitality, for, in the Twenty-first Dynasty Amenhotep III is reported in a decree carved on a limestone stela (now in the British Museum) to have visited the mortuary temple.[18] The king established a regular funerary cult for Amenhotep "in recognition of his perfect character." The text seems

90

to be a copy of an original document made to renew the old prerogatives of Amenhotep's priests and to guarantee their income.

During the Third Intermediate Period, the cult of Amenhotep
apparently declined steadily at the mortuary temple; at least no trace
of it has been found. At Karnak, however, Amenhotep continued to
be venerated during his lifetime and then more and more into the
Twenty-second Dynasty—more than five hundred years after his
death. Then, he was acclaimed by the priest and supervisor of the
doorway of the temple of Amun, named Hor-akh-bit, in a hieratic

Fig. 55. Amenhotep as an artist. Ostracon

text written on the wall north of the rooms of Hatschepsut in the inner temple of Amun at Karnak.[19] Hor-akh-bit gives a list of his ancestors through seventeen generations; then he addresses Amenhotep, Son-of-Hapu to confirm the authenticity of his ancestry:

> O Amenhotep, in your great and august name you know the secret powers in the writings of the past which date from the time of the ancestors.

The Egyptians have repeated almost exactly "the secret powers in the writings of the past" from the biographical inscriptions on Amenhotep's statues at Karnak. Also, he remembers "his great august name" for his intellectual qualities, especially for his knowledge of the writings, the literature.

In the early Twenty-sixth Dynasty the Egyptians mention a chapel of Amenhotep in western Thebes.[20] This was perhaps a poor successor to his mortuary temple. But, the Egyptians carved a standing male figure of Amenhotep soon after, in the reign of Psammetikh I (the base is now in Brooklyn.[21]) It is an important document that indicates the popularity of Amenhotep. On the base we read:

> O noble Amenhotep, Son-of-Hapu, justified! Come, good physician! Look, I suffer from my eyes. May you cause that I be healthy at once. I have made this as recompense for it, I, the king's daughter and princess, sweet in love, Merit-Neith, in the year 37 of the Good God, the lord of rituals, Psammetikh, given life eternally.

A daughter of Psammetikh is addressing Amenhotep, the "good physican," about some trouble with her eyes and dedicates the statue, apparently representing Amenhotep himself and designed for his cult place, to cure the disability. And the position of the epithet of "justified" after his name in the inscription reminds us of the tradition the Egyptians followed of placing *épithètes postposés* after the names of deified kings. All this proves that the Egyptians accepted Amenhotep as a well-known, established figure in religious life, especially as a famous healer. In addition, the fact that members of the royal family have recourse to this "saint" indicates that Amenhotep had a proportionately greater importance as a "saint" among the common people.

The Egyptians placed increasingly more of their faith in

Fig. 56. Base of a statue of Amenhotep, Saite
period

Amenhotep from the beginning of the Ptolemaic period onwards. Then, Manetho mentions Amenhotep in his history, written about 220 B.C., in relation to an event that occurred during the reign of Amenhotep III:

> King Amenophis wanted to see the gods as Hor did, one of his predecessors on the king's throne. And he told his wish to his namesake, Amenophis, whose father is Paapis, and who, on behalf of his wisdow and his knowledge of the future, was considered to share in divine nature.[22]

Amenophis, Son-of-Paapis is nobody else than Amenhotep, Son-of-Hapu; his father's name has the article **p3**.[23]

Amenhotep is named in religious literature, that is, in Ptolemaic versions of the *Book of the Dead* coming from Thebes. In a rubric to chapter 167, the circumstances under which the chapter was found are described:

> The book of the pot which was found by the first king's son Khaemwese under the head of a mummy in the west of Memphis.

> The book of one whose appearance is hidden, which was found by the king's chief scribe [in one textual variant: king's chief lector-priest], Amenhotep, Son-of-Hapu, the justified, and which he made himself as a protection for his limbs.[24]

There is an apparent contradiction in these passages; first, the Egyptians credited Khaemwese with finding the text, but then they give the credit to "the king's chief scribe."[25]

During the second and first century, Amenhotep's followers gave his priests and cult officials titles which indicated the important roles they expected the saint to fulfill:

> Priest of the house of all decisions of the king's scribe, Amenhotep, Son-of-Hapu. Priest of all decisions and all prescriptions of the king's scribe Amenhotep, Son-of-Hapu.[26]

In these titles Amenhotep's importance as a giver of oracles is clearly expressed.

Most of the documents concerning the worship of Amenhotep

94

originated in the area of Thebes (his chapels can be located from these same documents as being situated at Deir el-Bahari).[27] That this is the case is confirmed by the building inscription of the Ptolemaic chamber constructed by Ptolemy VIII, in the ruined temple of Hat-shepsut, where the sanctuary of Amenhotep is described as a renewal of an old one called **m3r.t.**[28]

In one of these documents, dating from the time of Ptolemy VI, the Egyptians referred to Amenhotep for the first time as "the great god."[29] The cult had come to be supported by a large number of followers, which is indicated by the number of people listed on a Green ostracon of the second century B.C.[30] The popularity of the cult is also indicated by the fact that we know of a large number of votive statues, offering tables, ostraca.

All of these documents indicate that Amenhotep served as a healer through oracles:

> I asked the great god Amenhotep. He answered that a fever was in the body of Teos and that two Syrian figs may be given to him, watered from the evening to the morning. . . . The liquid shall be poured in a vessel with broken bread and mixed well. He shall drink this and shall continue for four days.

The god gave him a (. . .) snake of iron, in order to tie it on his arm. There is no failure in it.[31] Amenhotep also was called upon to provide children. In a demotic letter dating from the early Ptolemaic Period, The priest Osoeris prays to

> . . . his master, the royal scribe Amenhotep, Son-of-Hapu, the great god . . .

for providing a child.

> If it happens, that Tai-pet [the hopeful mother] becomes preg-nant, I shall give him one deben. If it happens, that she give birth to a child, I shall give one more deben; together two deben for the good treatment. My great lord! This good scribe! Hear me, hear my voice! I am your servant and the son of your servant, since the beginning. Don't forget Osoeris. . . .[32]

(We also can see from this inscription that Amenhotep may be a "great god," but he is not *so* great, for Osoeris does not feel that he

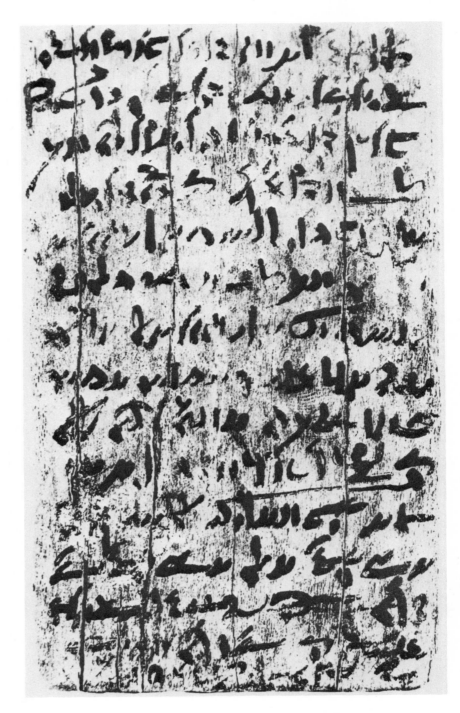

Fig. 57. Letter addressed to Amenhotep

must offer up everything before he is granted all of his wishes, and he can address the saint in an almost familiar way.)

Amenhotep had been revered by the Egyptians for many years as the source of respite from their physical ills. As I have mentioned before in this chapter, the Egyptians called upon Amenhotep to cure their physical ailments as early as the time of the reign of Amenhotep III, and they regarded him as a god and a healer even before that, when Ptolemy II was king. We have a Greek ostracon dating from this period from Deir el-Bahari that illustrates this:

> But I had heard from different sides that the miracles of Amenotes were numerous, that he was merciful and that the hopeless were numerous who had found curing by him. Being a hopeless case, I went along to the sanctuary of Amenotes as a suppliant. Amenotes helped me, and cured by him by a vision and having regained my health, I wished to express to him and the other gods sharing in his altars and cults their miraculous power in written words for those who visit the temple enclosure of Amenotes that they may see the power of this god when they are taken by any illness. . . .[33]

During the Hellenistic period, Amenhotep became renowned as a "sage" as well as a healer. Many moral statements, quite clearly of Greek origin, were ascribed to him and are known as "Counsels of Amenhotep."[34] We might guess that the followers of Amenhotep credited him with these sayings to propagate his popularity among the Greeks. And they must have been successful, for we know of a votive column that a Greek couple named Leon and Lysandra dedicated to Amenhotep in Deir el-Bahari in the time of Ptolmey VIII as recompense for the birth of a child.[35]

The Egyptians represented Amenhotep on the right wall of the Ptolemaic chapel deep in the rock behind the upper temple of Hatshepsut at Deir el-Bahari, facing the scene portraying Imhotep.[36] And, corresponding to Imhotep on the left wall, Amenhotep stands next to the door looking at it and facing an emblem of the town of Thebes (its hieroglyph is filled with thirty-seven stars, which may represent the number of temples located there). Amenhotep appears in an iconographic style similar to that of the contemporaneous statues of his lifetime: the long rounded wig and apron going up to his breast. This will be stereotyped in almost all of his representations made in Ptolemaic times. And from this time on the Egyptians com-

Fig. 58. Ptolemaic room in the temple of Hetshepsut. Amenhotep on the right wall

plete his insignia with the papyrus roll and the scribes' palette (although the palette is not included here). Again, the Egyptians call him

The royal scribe and chief scribe of the recruits, the sage Amenhotep, son of the living herald Apis, priest of Amun, his beloved, strong in his heart, issued from Seschat, divine offspring of Toth. . . .

Amenhotep has now become truly divine. He retains his earthly titles, but his father Hapu has become Apis. His mother also has become a deity; she is called

98

Hathor-Idit, the justified, the god's mother of the helpful god who has issued from her at this beautiful day, the 11th of Phamenoth, in her name "rejoicing."

The Egyptians transformed Amenhotep's parents into divinities, but they also gave him divine, *spiritual,* parents, Seschat and Toth.

Amenhotep's importance to the Egyptians as a god is clearly expressed in an inscription carved on the rear wall of the chamber:

> strong wall of iron to protect Egypt; Great lector-priest who conducts the temples of Egypt;

> follower of Toth, born by the nobleman Hapu, son of Amun, beloved by his heart; who gives life to men and women.[37]

Amenhotep now enjoys the fatherhood of Amun as well as that of Hapu. Amun has chosen Amenhotep to be his representative on earth, as is indicated in the epithet "beloved of his heart" quoted above. And, finally, the Egyptians hail Amenhotep as the

> divine offspring of the Lord of Hermopolis, protector of the Theban throne.

on the portico in front of the chamber.

The religious activity at this place, after the cult of Amenhotep and Imhotep is established in the rock chapel, is reflected in numerous votive inscriptions that were written on the walls of the portico by visitors to the chapel, as well as in the chambers and on the ruined buildings around the upper court of the temple of Hetshepsut. There are also a small number of demotic texts, which are the same as the normal type of votive inscriptions:

> The good name of PN may remain here in front of the royal scribe and scribe of the recruits Amenhotep, Son-of-Hapu, the great god.[39]

About two hundred votive inscriptions in Greek have survived to our time.[40] They were written up until the end of the second century A.D. by Greek pilgrims to the shrine. Almost all of the prayers are carved into the walls of some covered rooms adjoining the upper terrace of the temple of Hetshepsut. Some of the more typical texts

99

from the upper terrace should be mentioned. The first was of the type:

> Adoration of PN in front of our lord
> Amenothes [and in front of Asklepios].

The Macedonian worker Andromachos writes:

> I came to Amenothes, the helpful god. I fell ill, and the god cured me the same day.[41]

A short prayer of Eugraphis in front of

> . . . our lord, the god Asclepius, Amenothes and Hygieia[42]

provoked a Christian monk to add a closed ring of crosses around the text and to add

> One is our god, and he is our saviour.

A last example:

> I come from Coptos, I, Athenodoros, to the sanctuary of Asclepius and of Amenothes. During my prayers to the good Asclepius, the famous Amenothes and the very great goddess Hygieia, it happened that I heard. . . .[43]

A devotion that is more Egyptian than Greek was inscribed at Medinet Habu that simply refers to Amenhotep as "the scribe Amenhotep." But he is shown in an especially full divine costume with rounded wig, long beard, short apron, the life sign and scepter.[44]

We can assume that the pilgrims slept there in order to experience visions and receive cures through their dreams (this practice is mentioned several times in the inscriptions themselves).

Gradually, the people of Thebes accepted Amenhotep into their official pantheon, as they had Imhotep. Amenhotep enters the theology of the Ptolemaic temples first at Dier el-Medinah in the time of Ptolemy VI. We can see him on one of the columns of the small hypostyle hall with his normal attributes of a long apron, a long rounded wig, and a short beard.[45] The accompanying text calls him

Fig. 59. Column in the ptolemaic temple of Deir el-Medineh.
Amenhotep and his mother

The royal scribe and chief scribe of the recruits Amenhotep, son
of the nobleman Hapu, the justified, servant of Amun, beloved
of his heart, distinguished by him for his good character on
earth, whose name stays forever and will not perish eternally.

Behind him is his mother wearing the life sign and a crown that
queens wore during the time of the New Kingdom and later. She is
identified as

. . . the god's mother, the good nurse Itit, mistress of beauty.

101

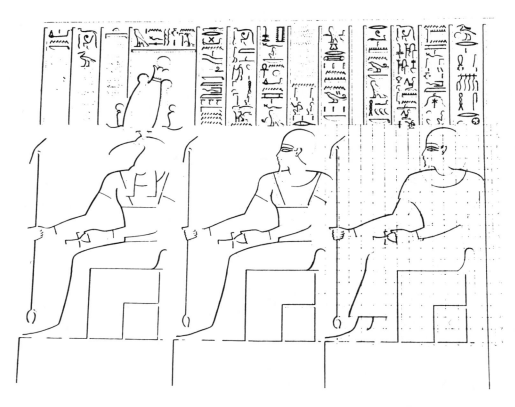

Fig. 60. Imhotep and Amenhotep in the temple of Qasr el-Aguz

At the end, the worshippers make an offering:

> . . . a boon which king gives for your *ka,* royal scribe Amenhotep, justified, consisting in thousands of good and pure things, coming from the offering-altar of Amun, that you may live by them every day.

Some Egyptians at this stage might have considered Amenhotep, like Imhotep, as a mortal, but because he was mortal he had an especial attractiveness and was held to be an effective saint. His holiness and divinity are not the fabrications of late times; they grew slowly out of his funerary cult and were more deeply connected with historical fact than were Imhotep's.

Both Amenhotep and Imhotep are represented as *truly divine* in a temple at Qasr el-Aguz, south of Medinet Habu.[46] The temple was built by Ptolemy VIII and was dedicated to a special form of the

102

wisdom god Toth and his formerly human colleagues Imhotep and Amenhotep. One of the main scenes in the temple shows Imhotep:

> . . . the helpful god . . ., master of life, giving life to everybody who loves him, who hears the prayers of the suffering, who takes care of any illness.[47]

Behind him is Amenhotep:

> the intelligent, issued from Seschat, of effective speech like the lord of Heseret [Toth].

The iconography distinguishes the two saints clearly. Amenhotep follows the pattern of his human appearance. But no gradual differentiation is made, for, in a small relief at the temple entrance, Amenhotep is suddenly shown wearing the crescent and moon disc—a clear assimilation to Thoth.[48] (This close identification of Amenhotep with Toth may be the reason why different classical scholars, such as Clement of Alexandria, mention, as typical deified mortals, "the Memphite Imhotep" and "the Theban Hermes."[49])

Finally, we see Ptolemy VIII and the goddess Wadjet entering the Ptolemaic rooms in the old temple of Tod.[50] They are preparing to make offerings to Tjenenet, the main goddess of this temple, and to Imhotep and Amenhotep. Imhotep is called

> . . . the helpful god; there is nobody like him to banish any illness from their bodies.

The Egyptians describe Amenhotep as the

> . . . son of the master of birth, the living, and the lady Itit

and of the divine father Apis and the human mother. And he is

> . . . the good physician through the existence of Maat, at the sight of whom injustice is removed.

There are many objects from western Thebes that are devoted to the veneration of both Amenhotep and Imhotep, but in most Imhotep is subordinate to Amenhotep. We have found only two documents to date in which they are treated as equals, in one instance on

Fig. 61. Imhotep and Amenhotep in the ptolemaic temple of Tôd

the Papyrus Boulaq 3, dating from the middle of the first century A.D. We read:

> Your soul will go to the royal scribe and chief scribe of the recruits Amenhotep; your soul will be united with Imhotep as soon as you are in the inner part of the valley. Your heart will be cheerful . . . and you will feel like a son in the house of his father.[50]

One of the great hopes of the Egyptians was to be united with Amenhotep and Imhotep in the after life. They would feel safe in their companionship, as at home. Apparently Amenhotep and Imhotep are taken here as gods of the dead. The other document is a limestone stela from Luxor which shows Imhotep and Amenhotep facing each other. Both are implored "to protect this house."

At about the same time that Amenhotep was being deified in western Thebes and then becoming associated with Imhotep, he also was being deified and becoming associated with Imhotep by the people of Karnak. Thus, Amenhotep and Imhotep are worshipped in the temple of Ptah in Karnak and then in the temple of Amun, as well as in north Karnak. The Egyptians finally established the interrelationship of Amenhotep and Imhotep with each other by carving a long hymn to Amenhotep on the fourth gate of the temple of Ptah at Karnak and another hymn to Imhotep on the other doorjamb.[52]

This text, dating from the time of Tiberius, is the latest and most detailed document that describes Amenhotep's worship at Thebes, and it recapitulates all of the information we can get from 1500 years of tradition:

> You are built by Ptah as his youthful repetition; he unites you with his community of gods; he provided you a rich income; he appointed you to be an advisor; he brought you up as the guard of the writings; he made you the companion of Toth, who knows the accounts better than the board which is in office. Your *ka* is a god to give life and health to everybody. You give a child to the sterile; you release a man from his enemy; you know the hearts of men and what is inside; you increase the lifetime; there is no distress in you. You renew what has fallen down; you fill up what was found destroyed. Your beloved son Tiberius reminds you.

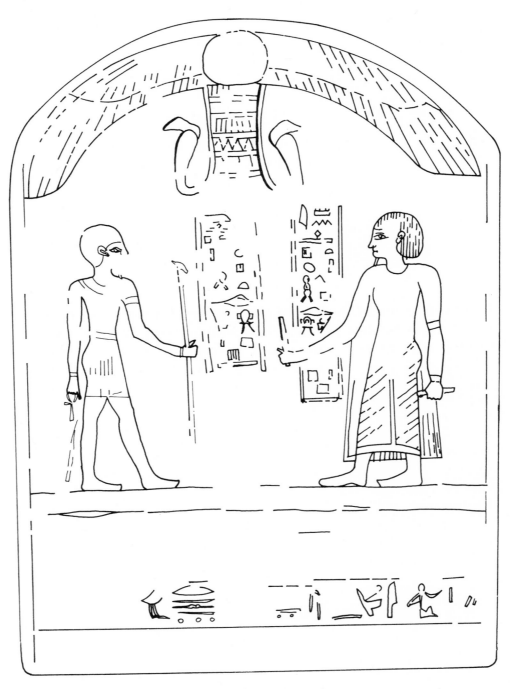

Fig. 62. Altar stela

The Egyptians erected the most monumental memorial to Amenhotep in Ptolemaic times in front of the right wing of the first pylon at the great temple of Amun at Karnak. It is a colossus more than four meters tall representing Amenhotep with his usual rounded wig and royal apron supported by a back pillar surmounted by a pyramidion on a high base. The conventional epithets and titles are carved on the figure and the base.[53] The inscription on the belt identifies the figure as

> The royal scribe and chief scribe of the recruits Amenhotep, Son-of-Hapu from the nome of Athribis.

A long series of titles is inscribed on the base, a rather fictive collection that could be found in Ptolemaic Times. This is followed by divine epithets:

> Divine offspring of the lord of Hermopolis, sensible in his heart, issued from Seschat, excellent in his speech like Imhotep, Son-of-Ptah, servant of Amun, chosen by him, the favorite of everybody.

The text on the back pillar explains why this statue was erected. Amenhotep himself is speaking:

> O Amun, may you grant that this statue endures in your temple. May you grant that I receive offerings from your altar every day like the statues of the nome-gods.
> I was the servant of the king Nab-maat-Re-Amenophis. He rewarded me more than the great nobles; he exalted me to his brothers, and I was a real pupil of the king, favorite in the palace and praised on behalf of the greatness of my excellence. I am on the water of the lord of the gods. I restored everything lost in the words of the gods; I made clear what was hidden in the holy books. He has given me gifts for years; he erected me huge statues in front of his majesty.

The statue belongs to the Ptolemaic period, and, as B. V. Bothmer has pointed out, this large figure, as well as all of the other colossal figures that were carved at this time were supposed to convey the superhuman nature of the subject being portrayed.[54] Amenhotep had been truly deified.

Fig. 63. Colossus of Amenhotep
from Karnak

To recapitulate, Amenhotep began his career as a simple official in the provinces of the delta. But because he possessed unusual personal qualifications, he eventually was summoned to the royal court where he soon made an impression on the intellectual life of the Egyptians. The Egyptians slowly equated his importance to the intellectual life of Egypt with an influence on religious matters. They began to consider Amenhotep as an intermediary with Amun. The simple people really began to look upon Amenhotep as a god because they appreciated the typically Egyptian qualities he personified; they thought of him as an individual who was hard working, technically skillful, clever in politics and even sly, loyal to the king, and deeply religious. He provided the people a kind of simple, uncomplicated divinity, and he assured himself of a memory that lasted for centuries.

NOTES

1. General bibliography: K. Sethe in *Festschrift Ebers* (1897), 107–116; W. R. Dawson, *Aegyptus* 7 (1926), 113–138.

2. The textual evidence is collected by A. Varille, *Inscriptions concernant l'architecte Amenhotep Pils de Hapou* (1968).

3. To be published by L. Habachi in *RdE*.

4. For the general historical background see W. C. Hayes in *CAH* II/I (1973) 338ff.; E. Riefstahl, *Thebes in the Time of Amunhotep III* (1964).

5. See note 2 above.

6. Cario CG 583/835 (Varille, *o.c.*, pl. 5–8); CG 42127 (*ibid.*, pl. 1); CG 551 (*ibid.*, pl. 11); JE 36498 (*ibid.*, pl. 9–10).

7. Cairo JE 44861 (*ibid.*, pl. 4); JE 44862 (*ibid.*, pl. 3).

8. *PM* VII, 170 (5)–(6); A. Varille, *o.c.*, 61–63, fig. 5–6, no. 26.

9. *PM* II², 456; D. Bidoli, *MDAIK* 26 (1970) 11-14, pl. 7.

10. A. Varille, *o.c.* 104–106, no. 38–39; D. Bidoli, *o.c.*, 11, fig. 1.

11. H. Carter, *JEA* 4 (1917), 114, no. 251, pl. 19; E. Thomas, *Royal Necropoleis of Thebes* (1966), 160, fig. 16, 179–180, pl. 44 B, 45 A.

12. *PM* II², 456; A. Varille, *o.c.*, 113–120, pl. 13–14.

13. *PM* II², 455; C. Robichon-A. Varille, *Le temple du scribe royal Amenhotep fils de Hapou* (1936); A. Varille, *Inscriptions . . .*, 65–66, 86–103, 138–139; fig. 7, 12-24.

14. *PM* 1², 107–108 (4); A. Varille, *o.c.*, 121–123, no. 56, pl. 12.

15. *PM* I², 422 (4); A. Varille, *o.c.* 106–107, fig. 29.

16. Berlin 21447; A. Varille, *o.c.*, 106–107, fig. 28.

17. Pap. Brit. Mus. 10053; E. Peet, *The Great Tomb Robberies* (1930), 108, 119, pl. 19, 21; Pap. Brit. Mus.

10054: *ibid.*, 64, 65, pl. 7, 8; Pap. Brit. Mus. 10068: *ibid.*, 96, pl. 15.

18. Brit. Mus. 138: A. Varille, *o.c.*, 67–85, no. 27.

19. *PM* II², 103 (306). W. Spiegelberg, *PSBA* 24, (1902), 320-324.

20. Pap. Louvre 2432 I.4 M. Malinine, *Choix de textes juridiques* (1953), 102–103, 106, n.5

21. H. Wild, *MDAIK* 16 (1958), 406–413, pl.23.

22. W. G. Waddell (ed.), *Manetho* (1964), 120–125.

23. Cf. A. Erman, *ZÄS* 15 (1877), 147–148. G. Manteuffel, *De opusculis graecis Aegypti e papyris, ostracis lapidibusque collectis* (1930), 29–33, 99–106.

24. Pap. Louvre 3248, Pap. Leiden T. 31: see P. Barguet, *Le Livre des Morts* (1967), 240.

25. For Khaemwese and his role as a *Memphite hero, see now* F. Gomaà, *Chaemwese, Sohn Ramses' II und Hoherpriester von Memphis* (1973), 71, 94 (no. 99), 96 (no. 112), 134, fig. 34.

26. See e.g. *Prosopographia Ptolemaica* III, 61, no. 5436; G. Botti, *L'archivio demotico da Deir elmedineh* (1967), 122–123, 132–133, 174–175, 181–182.

27. Cf. M. Malinine, *Choix de textes juridiques,* (1953), 106, n.5; G. Botti, *o.c.,* 121–122, 132-134.

28. See n. 67, Chapter 20

29. *Pap. Dem.* Brit. Mus. 10230: N. Reich, *Papyri juristischen Inhalts* (1934), 78–79, 82.

30. J.-G. Milne, "Greek Texts," in *Theban Ostraca* (1913), 158–159, no. 142.

31. H. Thompson, *PSBA* 35 (1913), 95–96, pl. 27.

32. M. Malinine, *RdE* 14, (1962), 37–43, pl. 2.

33. Cairo JE 67300: P. Guéraud, *BIFAO* 27 (1927), 121-125; A. Bataille, *Etudes de Papyrologie* 4 (1938), 125-131, pl. 3.

34. Ostracon from Deir el-Bahari: U. Wilcken in *Festschrift Ebers* (1897), 142–146.

35. Cairo CG 9304: G. Milne, *Greek Inscriptions* (1905), 37, no. 9304, pl. 4.

36. *PM* II², 368 (147); E. Naville, *The Temple of Deir el-Bahri* V (1906), pl. 150.

37. *PM* II², 368 (148); I am indebted to Ph. Derchain for a full copy of the inscriptions of this wall.

38. *PM* II², 365 (127).

39. Some published by W. Spiegelberg, *Demotica* II (1928), 28–29.

40. A. Bataille, *Les inscriptions grecques du temple de Hatshepsout a Deir el-Bahair* (1951).

41. *Ibid.,* no. 48.

42. *Ibid.,* no. 86.

43. *Ibid.,* no. 126.

44. W.F. Edgerton, *Medinet Habu Graffiti Facsimiles* (1937), pl. 5, no. 19.

45. *PM* II², 402 (9).

46. D. Mallet, *Le Kasr el-Aguz* (1909).

47. *PM* II², 528 (2).

48. *PM* II², 527 (1).

49. *Stromateis* I 21, 314.1.

50. Unpublished. A copy of the texts made by G. Posener was kindly provided by S. Sauneron.

51. J.-Cl. Goyon, *Rituels funéraires de l'ancienne Égypte* (1972), 52-53.

52. *PM* II², 197 (4) (c).

53. Cairo CG 1199: *PM* II², 22.

54. *Egyptian Sculpture of the Late Period* (1960), 127.